REVIVING

THE SPIRIT

REVIVING THE SPIRIT

A Generation of African Americans

Goes Home to Church

BEVERLY
HALL LAWRENCE

Grove Press
New York

Published simultaneously in Canada
Printed in the United States of America
FIRST EDITION

Library of Congress Cataloging-in-Publication Data

Lawrence, Beverly Hall.
Reviving the spirit : a generation of African Americans goes home to church / Beverly Hall Lawrence. — 1st ed.
p. cm.
ISBN 0-8021-1562-4
1. Afro-Americans—Religion. 2. Afro-Americans—Biography.
3. Spiritual biography. I. Title.
BR563.N4L37   1996
277.3'0829'08996073—dc20   95-38857

DESIGN BY LAURA HAMMOND HOUGH

Grove Press
841 Broadway
New York, NY 10003

10 9 8 7 6 5 4 3 2 1

For my Father who art in Heaven

and

My husband, Calvin, my light on Earth

CONTENTS

CONTENTS

IN THE BEGINNING

A Prologue

Write, therefore, what you have seen, what is now and what
will take place later.
—*Revelation 1:19*

I couldn't remember exactly how I had "lost my religion," as my grandma, Maude "Mama" Lewis, would have summed up my lukewarm relations with God at the time. It hadn't been a sudden or shocking loss, not like losing your wallet at the mall or anything. Nor was it a mysterious loss, like when you're positive two socks went into the wash but only one comes out. I suppose it was because of Mama that at twenty-nine I was still thinking of religion in that way—as a *thing*, something to possess or be possessed by, which I neither had nor was at the moment.

For Mama's generation, and pretty much for my mom's too, religion seemed fairly black or white—you either had it or you didn't. And as best as I could tell, "having religion" revealed itself in regular church attendance, saying nightly prayers, and instinctively yelling "Thank You Jesus" in moments of unexpected good fortune, or "Lord Have Mercy" in times of trouble. "Losing your religion" could mean, at worst, that you possessed hopelessly weak moral fiber, yielded to temptations (a.k.a. sinning), and too often had idle hands, the devil's very workshop. Then there were those who lost their religion—evidenced by irregular church attendance and skipping nightly prayers—those who could just as easily have been said to have simply lost interest in religion or gone lax in attending church, that place where I thought we "got religion."

I grew up in Mama's house on Story Street in Ashburn, Georgia, with my older sister, Natalie, and my mom, Eunice Lewis Hall, until "Eun" married my new dad, Howard Michael Gaither, "Sonnie," when I was twelve. Mama and Eun were both decidedly Southern and Baptist, with all the rural traditional implications, and my rearing was in their "yes ma'am, no ma'am," spirit. Ours were not "religious" households by any stretch. But I do remember that as little girls, most nights, after we'd been scrubbed, dusted white with Johnson's Baby Powder, and dressed in matching pajamas, it was on our knees we'd go: "Now I lay me down to sleep. . . . If I should die before I wake, I pray to the Lord my soul to take. . . ." And we always said grace as a family before all meals, which meant twice a day, at breakfast and dinner. "God is great, God is good, let us thank Him for this food" was such a part of mealtime rites, I thought it a component of good table manners, like waiting until everyone is served before eating, not an act of religious gratitude.

There was, of course, a Holy Bible in Mama's house. And although we learned early on that it was a book of stories, I understood right away that it was different from all the other books around the house in a family of mostly school

4

teachers and principals. Mama's Bible in size alone commanded respect, having the shape and heft of a large-city telephone book with pages of King James language printed in large type full of *thous* and *wilts*. It had been a gift to Mama from her children—Eun, my aunt Whilomenia "Mena" Bennett, and my uncle George "Brother" Lewis Jr.—and was covered in black leather, the lettering embossed in metallic gold. It was never called the Family Bible, but it was. I don't remember us reading from it in a formal way, but I sometimes looked at the pictures, vibrant ink drawings printed on parchment with fancy script writing and pages rimmed in gold. The names of all Mama's children, grandchildren, and everybody before them, too, had been neatly inked in blue in the front, so I also understood early on that the Bible was more than the Word of God: it was a safe haven, a safety deposit box for records considered important for all time. Mama's Bible was kept in its own special place, the end table nearest the front door of her white-frame house, alongside stacks of *Ebonys* and *Jets* and *Guideposts*. There were not many other visible Christian symbols, no portraits of Jesus save the ones on cardboard fans given to us by the insurance men. There was one kind of religious portrait, in which an angel in full, flowing robes floated over a pair of little white children as they made their way over a bridge during a thunderstorm. I suppose this image reflected my understanding of the function of God and his heavenly hosts: to watch over children lost during a storm to make sure they got home safely.

You could say that I was raised in the church, as were most of my friends. I made Jesus' acquaintance when I, too, was a babe swaddled in Eun's arms, and went on to attend Sunday School from kindergarten to high school graduation, where I recited my share of Easter speeches, acted in church plays, attended church-sponsored picnics and out-of-town trips to Six Flags over Georgia adventure land park, and sat through many a full-length sermon preached by the Reverend J. J. ("Can I get an Amen?") Johnson at New Providence Baptist Church in Ashburn.

Since in that worldview, church was the place where you got religion, I suppose I began to lose mine the day I stopped going to that place. Following the traditional path of leaving the parents' nest, I left home, Ashburn, and New Providence for Atlanta, two hundred miles north, to attend Morris Brown College after I graduated from high school. And though I had learned it was the duty of a Christian forced to leave the home church to reunite with another body as soon as possible, the idea of going to church sort of slipped from significance. As the distance grew between New Providence and me, my relationship with church began to lose its luster. It was not unlike what happens to some friendships that fade when one moves away or the ties that once bound begin to unravel. It is not always a lack of desire or sincerity, but sometimes the distance is too great, and empty space sets up a convenient barrier. My relationship with God, too, seemed to fade as the distance widened between me and the church where I first got religion.

In the Beginning: A Prologue

Whoever believes and is baptized will be saved . . .

—Mark 16:16

On such a spirit-filled day, it was completely understandable that memories and mixed feelings overflowed as my mind raced back over the ten years that had passed since I left home and New Providence. I thought about the path that had led me 360 degrees to Shiloh Baptist Church, where I'd come to witness my husband, Calvin Perry Lawrence Jr., get religion. It was gloriously sunny on the fourth Sunday in April, the 22nd, 1990, and "angels were smiling in heaven," a deacon had said of this, "a great going down mornin'." We were about sixty in all in the basement of a tiny red brick church in Jamaica, Queens, one of thousands of long-serving churches in the thousands of neighborhoods that make up New York City. It was nearly two in the afternoon, immediately following a traditional worship service my friend Katti Gray described as "straight out the briar patch," meaning it had down home appeal, and could just as easily have been given in my New Providence Baptist Church in Ashburn. She was there, as was Mira Thomas, another friend, and Calvin's parents, Ursula and Calvin Lawrence, all invited to witness him being born again.

We were gathered in the rear near a ceramic-tiled wading pool. All around the pool were faces that had become familiar in the six months we had been coming to Shiloh. Among the gaggle of deaconesses were Sister Ethel Pearson, "Mother" of the church, Sister Mabel Whitaker, and her son

Quincy Brooks, who had first so warmly welcomed us to Shiloh and was to become on this day our new "brother" in Christ. Many of the older sisters who gathered around smelling of pomade and Ben Gay were dressed mostly in white, and many graying heads were crowned with Sunday-go-to-meeting hats. The pianist struck a chord, and joyful wails and moans pleaded all around . . ."Take me to the water. . . ," "Nothing but the blood. . . ," and "Saved a wretch like me."

Some were standing on folding chairs to gain better vantage, others were clinging to the shaky wrought-iron railing ringing the pool, which was about the size of a hot tub in any fitness center, with about as much water. Its design required you to climb up a few steps and ease yourself down into the water. There on the edge of the pool Calvin was standing, looking a bit like a mummy draped in endless folds of white, completely wrapped in two white bed sheets, as were the other candidates for baptism. Calvin was the tallest and the last of seven sinners, six of whom had gone down before him. He lowered himself into the clear, cold water until he came face to face with Pastor Alvin Tunstill Jr., a young man not much older than him, until they stood waist deep in what turned into a modern-day River Jordan, that stream that flows to bathe the growing tide of believers. In Christian faith, the baptism is among the most powerful of religious rituals, a real and symbolic washing away of sin. Images of Jesus being baptized by John in the River Jordan flashed back from those parchment pages in Mama's Bible. This was something truly ancient.

In a way, I envied that Calvin had waited until he was an adult to make this symbolic covenant with Christ. His decision to get baptized at thirty-one constituted a whole different approach to the altar of God than mine, for that reason alone. I respected his desire to get washed in the water and to have the chance to be reborn. When I made the decision to be baptized, I wasn't a consenting adult. For me, baptism was a traditional rite of passage. In the church where I grew up, almost everyone had "become a member" by the age of twelve. To have not done so showed either orneriness or— something that I didn't even think about—an *opinion* about religious expression. Everyone I knew back then was "god-fearing." Whether they went to church or not, they had joined one, confessed their sins, and been baptized. Calvin's and my upbringings were not so different. His parents were of the same Southern tradition as mine, and he, too, was raised in the church. But he was never forced to join, so he didn't. I was not "forced" to join either, but I do not remember my own baptism at eight as soul stirring, as Calvin's seems.

When I was growing up, each summer our church would have a week devoted to evangelism, a time we called having revival. Perhaps because of the festive spirit, during revival was a time when youngsters seemed to join, and I was no different—even though my mom assures me that I was as strong willed then as I am now and that I made the decision quite independently and in my own time. It seems that my sister and all my friends had joined the church en masse a year earlier during summer revival. Eun and my aunt Lois, Brother's wife, cried when I joined the church, going up all by myself to sit on the Mourner's Bench, the place where sinners contemplate what it will mean to confess their sins before they are baptized.

Pastor Alvin stood with one hand over Calvin's face and the other around his waist. In the name of the Father, the Son, and the Holy Ghost, he dunked Calvin, and the sisters shouted "Thank-ya Jesus." They saw a soul saved, but I also saw hope for the church to be born again. For Shiloh, my husband Calvin's baptism meant fresh blood, a transfusion of strength to fight the generational gap that threatens this church after 114 years.

I could not be baptized again, so I moved my membership to Shiloh from New Providence and with Calvin received the Right Hand (shake) of Fellowship, making us full members of the congregation and the body of Christ. We were officially back in the fold. They call me Sister Lawrence now. It sounds funny even to me. I am not a holy roller. I've never spoken in tongues and have not yet been visited by the Holy Ghost. Then again, I did not join the church to get to heaven. I joined to survive on earth.

I was glad when they said unto me, Let us go into the House of the Lord forever.

—Psalm 122:1

I wish I could say our path to Shiloh was the result of a divine sign or a deliberate search for a church home. There was never a sudden epiphany or a voice from a burning bush that kindled our desire to connect to a larger body.

It had begun, rather, on a dull Saturday in December in 1987, when Calvin announced that among his resolutions for the new year was to go back to church. We'd been married for about two years. Calvin was working as an editor for a small daily newspaper, the *Ann Arbor News*, and I was a reporter with the *Detroit Free Press*. Aside from getting married in New Providence in my hometown, religious expression had not yet entered our newly joined lives.

Spirituality was never missing in our lives, just some sort of formal expression of it. We'd always talked cosmically about the meaning of it all, you know, in the Zen, Jah Rastafari, creation vs. evolution way, right along with the possibility of space travel and the supernatural. "Thank the Lord" was just something we said "for good measure." Believing in a higher power was one thing; "going back to church" was another matter entirely.

In Ann Arbor, the handful of churches for African Americans tended to remind me of the ones I had left behind in Georgia. Traditional, reverential, Sunday clothes required, with the only reward being the chance to spend a couple of hours in the company of "real" black people. For relative strangers as we were, the churches felt oddly familiar and like a connection to a past that felt more secure. The services and rituals came as a needed tonic to cure this emptiness we were feeling.

Because journalism is a nomadic profession, within a short time, professional upheaval landed us in Washington, D.C., with me working at the *Washington Post* and Calvin at *USA Today*. As was becoming our custom, we made contact with the professional world through our jobs but with the "culture" of the city by seeking out a black church.

Our new church home was in a converted auditorium in Suitland, Maryland, a middle-class suburban enclave of Washington. A high school had loaned this space to a man of the cloth who was currently in the headlines as the "rene-gade" Roman Catholic priest, Father George Augustus Stall-ings. Father Stallings had become a kind of modern-day Christian soldier fighting to add an African-American spin on Catholic liturgy. He had become a lightning rod of contro-versy when the pope denied his request, and he broke with Rome, founding his own Imani Temple.

Services at Imani Temple were the rocking, soul-revival, make-a-joyful-noise kind that my soul needed, and I cheered this minister's defiance. I had grown up in churches waiting on the change to come, all solemn, sad, and dead. But here was a young man saying, "Whom shall I fear? My eyes are ever on the Lord, of Whom shall I be afraid?" It was this air of defiance as much as the spectacle of his masses that pulled us back week after week, when we'd go early enough to be seated near the altar, to smell the incense and see the perspiration on his brow. As a human vessel, Father Stallings may have been flawed, as his critics suggested, but for me he was a messenger with an Afro-specific message that was like silk in my ear. I was working in one of the "whitest" professions, and by Sunday I wanted the blackest experience I could find. It was while we were in D.C. that I began to see a possibility for the church to have dominion in my life.

Ask the former generations and find out what their fathers learned. For we were born only yesterday and know nothing.

—Job 8:8–9

By the time of Calvin's baptism in 1990, I had already witnessed hundreds of young black professionals like us join-ing churches in the communities where we'd lived. We had been witnesses to faith in Detroit, Ann Arbor, Washington, and now in New York City. In even the most casual social gatherings, there seemed to be questions about faith and discussions of how black churches might be the best spiritual, social, and economic hope for black America. In an essay recalling Calvin's baptism for *Newsday*, where we both now work, I equated our rejoining the church with an overt political statement or a nationalist, pro-black act. At the heart of the essay and of our intentions seemed a suggestion that we were part of a new generation of "believers" seeking to revive the church as an instrument of change. Our generation, it seemed, wanted to return to the historical roots of the church that had been led by our foreparents during each critical stage of racial progress from Emancipation to the movement for civil rights. When published, the essay generated a chorus of respondents who agreed with my soul's findings. For me, this was a further suggestion that something significant indeed was happening in African-American culture. It seemed a signal was beginning to sound for an entire generation, steering us back home to church. Put simply, the thousands of young blacks returning to the nation's 65,000 black churches truly constituted, as the *Washington Post* stated, "a movement sweeping through black middle-class congregations."

Statistically, African Americans are part of the larger return of baby boomers to religion. Cover stories in magazines and newspapers nationwide have chronicled the reviving spirituality of the postwar generation. This group of about sixty million Americans—the oldest of whom is approaching fifty—has been called by sociologist Wade Clark Roof "the generation that forgot God," because more than two-thirds—forty million—dropped out of churches and synagogues in the 1960s and 1970s.

Ours was truly the last "churched" generation, since most Americans born in the immediate postwar boom were raised in "religious" households. There are myriad reasons, personal and practical, that God seemed to become less significant for my generation. We came of age in the sixties and seventies, when Americans were struggling with how much civil and social liberty would be allowed in a brave new world. In the popular culture there was a general questioning of authority and of the traditional patterns of living, and the church was not exempt from that reevaluation.

The black church had been instrumental during the legal struggles for civil rights, but the role that the institution should play in African-American culture came into discussion at that time. My generation's early adult years were spent in an America that was literally on fire. The country was embroiled in the Vietnam War and its domestic protests at the same time it was trying to cope with the impact of integration. As we entered the seventies, the mood in some parts of the African-American community was growing more dispirited and angry as a result of the assassinations of Martin Luther King Jr. and Malcolm X. On college campuses, middle-class blacks were embracing a kind of intellectual and cultural attitude called black nationalism. At the same time, in urban centers, the black consciousness movement with its slogans "Black Is Beautiful" and "I'm Black and I'm Proud" was attracting followers with this same spirit of nationalism. Black America's cultural soul was on fire as well, and all our symbols were being questioned—including the white Jesus that we had bowed before during our childhoods. My generation was one that fled churches filled with those who appeared to us to be helpless, sitting and waiting for (a white) God to intervene and settle problems for them. Many of my friends and I admit now that at times the idea of going to church was simply too embarrassing, because it taught people to wait for change to come and because of its reliance on European Christian symbols.

As we mature, many of us now are looking back to what seems like "the good old days," to those traditional institutions like churches in hopes of finding guidance and a framework for living. Now that we're nearing middle age and are raising families, boomers are beginning to contemplate the meaning of life. We are returning, therefore, in part, because religion can provide a framework for basic questions regarding the origin, purpose, and meaning of life. Passage into middle age and the new spirituality, therefore, account for some of this revival of interest by blacks, but there are also indications that many are returning to the church in hopes of reviving its role as a command center and strategic outpost in our community.

Then come, let us go up to Bethel, where I will build an altar to God, who answered me in the day of my distress and who has been with me wherever I have gone.
—Genesis 35:3

It has come as a gradual and painful reality to those like me who thought that race would not matter much in our lives that it does. For my generation, the opportunity of fuller participation in certain areas of society and the attainment of greater economic resources have been liberating, but with the statistical failure of integration, the idea of assimilating has lost its luster for many. Most African Americans live in racially segregated communities, and social contact with whites is limited primarily to work relations. We've been to Martin's mountaintop and found it barely segregated—we feel accepted by whites at the office but not in their homes. We're together and reasonably comfortable during business hours, but at five o'clock we head home to neighborhoods kept segregated by redlining and habit. Physical separation has not made for casual socializing.

Ironically, those of us in the black middle class are physically isolated in two ways. There is the obvious separation between white and black American cultures and lifestyles, but also within the African-American community, those with higher incomes and education are finding themselves in a kind of limbo world—not really black or white—rather a super-black but lonely physical state of being. *Village Voice* essayist Nelson George has described those of us in this black middle class as being "separated by style, talk and taste and money from the boyz in the hood."

It has been a withering recognition for many African Americans as we've learned that successfully integrating too often requires a molting of any "blackness." To remain successful and sane, we've played a kind of "flipping" game, as we call it when you both play the white game and try to preserve your black soul. What is remarkable is that as our success in the white world has increased, our spiritual souls seem to have suffocated, and that despite gains and racial progress, we are basically on a high wire without a net.

The Lord spoke to Moses in the Tent of Meeting. . . .
Take a census of the whole community by their clans
and families, listing every man by name, one by one.
—Numbers 1:1–2

In preparing this book, I felt, of course, the need to quantify what I knew instinctively was happening—that a growing number of African Americans were returning to church as a home base. The church name that kept surfacing in my research was Bethel African Methodist Episcopal Church in Baltimore, Maryland. Initially, Bethel was among the churches featured in a *Time* magazine cover story exploring the growth in black middle-class churches. For me, it would take only one visit to Bethel, where I witnessed hundreds, thousands of young, proud, African-American folks like me wailing and falling on their knees, to know that I had found sufficient source material. I had been looking outside of New

York because of the "there's New York and there's the rest of country" kind of chauvinism. Not mine, but I knew New York wouldn't hold up as a slice of American apple pie. I had hoped for a church that would provide some good empirical support that was also a living example of what happens when people acting individually join with a congregation. Bethel was a godsend.

Baltimore is one of America's oldest and most beautiful cities. It still possesses much of its original, centuries-old architecture, and Bethel's cathedral is a fine example. Located on Druid Hill Avenue at the end of a block of red brick row houses, Bethel is an imposing limestone structure of gray and pink tones topped with Gothic spires that can be seen from downtown.

It is one of those large, flashy, influential churches that naturally folks put a "big" in front of: "Oh, you're talking 'bout Big Bethel," people say. Every major city and town has a church like Bethel in its African-American community, but Bethel in Baltimore is special because it is one of the oldest churches in the country and among the first established in the African Methodist Episcopal (AME) denomination—one of six that historically cater to African Americans.

Founded in 1785, Bethel is more than two hundred years old and has served primarily those in the African-American middle class. Black churches like Bethel have long served as the heart of life and social change in communities every- where. While many things have changed in recent decades, church hasn't. More than 71 percent of black churches are located where they were almost fifty years ago, and Bethel is no exception.

But churches like Bethel, that had served in prosperous, segregated black neighborhoods, began to find themselves obsolete in the mid-sixties, affected by the changing lifestyles and cultural attitudes of their members. By the early 1970s, one of Baltimore's largest black churches, Bethel found itself with only a few hundred active members.

The year Bethel came to my attention, in 1990, the church was garnering media and scholarly attention for spurts of growth in membership. That year, it ranked among the five fastest-growing congregations, black or white, in America and was called by scholar C. Eric Lincoln of Duke University, "the mother of the movement" in attracting younger members to the African Methodist Episcopal denomination. Bethel AME has climbed from 310 members in 1975 to nearly 10,000 today, and the average age of its members is now a relatively young thirty-five. The congregation is nearly 40 percent male, which is about twice the proportion in most black churches. Men and women drive long distances from the suburbs to attend one of three Sunday services in which about 1,500 worshippers vie for pew space. In its experimentation and results, Bethel is a microcosm of the dramatic changes taking place in black churches today. With highly educated laities and leaders, such churches are reshaping a traditional institution and making it relevant for those returning.

In the Beginning: A Prologue

Pray that I may proclaim it clearly, as I should.

—Colossians 4:4

The only song I can sing confidently is my own, and so this is my hymn about the spiritual soul of my generation. This is a story about how a generation weaned on the Lawd has come to make peace with its parents and the ole-time religion. We may have outgrown the neighborhood, but our spiritual voids were still there. Now, we are returning to look unto the hills whence cometh our help. This is for me a journal of faith, that of mine and of others who through independent acts have reattached themselves to the collective, the church family.

At Bethel, I found a chorus of voices sounding a familiar pitch that echoes from many others in the mainstream of this movement.

While in chronological age we vary some, our revelations seem to chime similar themes. We are products of a separate and unique American culture, and church seems to be one of the "black thangs" that we all understand. Each of us is on a solo journey to find our own faith—our own home—but recorded here are those echoes that I heard and felt when I encountered fellow spiritual travelers. Illustrating my generation's yearnings, the actions of those at Bethel will illuminate this movement back to church. Ultimately, for me what is validating about this book is that I have learned that I am organically and physically connected to a movement of people singing for their souls' salvation.

LOST IN THE PROMISED LAND

The First Chapter

We all, like sheep, have gone astray; each of us has turned to
his own way . . .
—*Isaiah 53:6*

It was not easy for her to pin-point exactly when the vanishing had begun, for it had not been sudden or something that simply had overtaken Pam Shaw in the night. We agreed, in fact, that "vanishing" described only the final part, really, that moment when she felt swallowed by feelings of worthlessness and uncertainty so consuming and confusing that she no longer recognized herself. "Vanished" may have been only a psychological realm where she lingered, but it seemed to Pam in her dispirited state that even her person was becoming null and void as well. The vanishing had not been so mercifully quick a disappearance as the word might suggest. For just as one could not possibly acquire in an instant the kind of spirited self-confidence that emanated from Pam today, neither could something so vital have been easily lost.

What Pam could recall more easily was the unending stress and anxiety of modern life that had slowly suffocated and strangled her sense of worth and purpose, the genesis of which could probably be traced to the days when she had moved to Baltimore as a young law student. She'd planned to fulfill her childhood dream of adding the word "Esquire" to her name as a member of the Maryland bar. That's when she first ran into trouble in the Promised Land.

Pam began losing sight of herself in 1982. The striking reflection she found each morning in the bathroom mirror would seem to start the day okay enough. Familiar almond-shaped eyes she dramatized with shadow and liner, eager and bright for someone past twenty-five. With skin the color of black coffee, hers was a face of high cheekbones and thinnish lips, features that some might describe as finely chiseled. Her hair had been styled by a barber's close cut into a high-top fade and was indeed a crowning touch. In profile, she could have been a modern Nefertiti, the Egyptian queen whose image in popular culture has become synonymous with black beauty.

"A fine sistah!" she would confidently reassure the reflection each day. For it must simply be the sun's rays that somehow betrayed all this that was so black and beautiful. Why else would her law school classmates at the University of Maryland not recognize her on the way to classes they shared, even after she'd given them a friendly wave? The blank stares or startled recognitions that sometimes came she at first took in stride as unfamiliarity between recent acquaintances. After all, like Pam, many were new to U of M's Baltimore campus and to studying law. But unlike her, the majority of the five hundred students were white. Pam was one among sixty African Americans.

As the months went by, many of her newer friendships were with these white classmates. But with time, she began to notice little things like the unreturned waves. "Little things" that made her feel that beyond campus, she lacked individual identity. That when she encountered these "friends" on the inner-city streets surrounding the campus, as an African-American woman in a largely black city she was unseen by them. A shadow to be passed silently in the night. She hated to sound like a broken Ralph Ellison record, but she felt invisible. "I went to a white college, grew up in a white high school, but I never experienced what I felt in law school," Pam recalls. "You'd sit in class with a white person all day long, and then you walk three blocks away from the school and they don't acknowledge you. I didn't understand this." What she sensed was not racial contempt from her white schoolmates but an indifference and dismissiveness that she felt was demeaning.

Shaken by her seeming transparency, she devised little "tests" of her personhood. One of these tests was kind of like the game of chicken—a kind of contest of bravery and dominance where dueling cars, for example, race headlong toward each other until one loses heart and swerves. In Pam's game of chicken, any white person who entered her path could become an opponent. Pam's chicken strategy would provide evidence for what she felt: that most white people simply pretend a black person is not present or visible and therefore will not swerve or veer to grant right of way to a black person. "White people will not move. If they see you coming, they won't move. Black people are always ducking and dodging." In her game of chicken, whites don't even think to blink. In grocery stores and other public places, she played chicken, refusing to duck and dodge and sometimes ending up with bruised shoulders. But what was worse, each game of chicken made her feel more like one.

Unfortunately, Pam says, her isolation was not confined to campus, for she was not making new friends of color either. Baltimore is a majority African-American city, and that was among the reasons she was attracted to it. But in spirit, it is a family town, and social bridges weren't easy to build for someone single and twenty-something. Still quaint and provincial, Baltimore didn't offer much in the way of clubs, theater, or places for casual socializing.

Eventually, even Pam didn't recognize the face in the mirror. "It was all the stuff that was completely unfamiliar to me that fed into each other. The lack of a support system, no friends, no family." Where was the determined face she remembered from when she was a little girl in Mississippi whose heart was set on being a lawyer and living "up north"? If this was her promised land, why couldn't she find in her face signs of joy divine?

The longing not to be "nothing" is among the sharpest hungers a human can know. It is not unlike the heart stab one feels in seeing one's own reflection fade from a lover's eye. But at times, even with those we know only casually—or not at all— this hunger not to be nothing can be just as crippling. To be denied a name or anything distinguishing is among the most dehumanizing of conditions—the death of the ego. It is a common tool of torturers of prisoners during war and of slavers in robbing the spirit of their captives. The need to be special, to stand out, is an urge we all feel. But it is an urge that is always in conflict and competition with another strong primal hunger: to belong, the desire for communality, to be part of a whole, the comfort that we are one among the many. To this can be added our society's belief that "standing out" and being recognized is somehow "good," and therefore that person is good by extension. If you go unrecognized, then, you must be "bad."

Most of us will mercifully never know loss of personhood in the extreme, but what of the many subtle ways in which each day we can be denied? The ego stings at slights, if only by a snooty store clerk or waiter. Dismissed. Dissed. "Acted like I wasn't even there," ". . . looked right through me," "I know she saw me." The hunger gnawing at Pam Shaw by the mid-1980s brought her to her knees in Bethel African Methodist Episcopal Church. Foremost among her pleas: "I am somebody! . . . aren't I?"

Jesus asked: "What is your name?"

—Luke 8:30

Though Southern in upbringing, Pam Shaw wouldn't fit any typecast of a country girl from the Mississippi Delta. She was in no way a shrinking violet, I thought after our meeting in 1993. I tried to contrast the woman filling my eyes with the self-reflection that she had shared. The woman I observed this Sunday morning moved with regal confidence through the crowd trying to find a seat at Bethel's 7:30 A.M. service. Her fit, athletic body was outfitted with the staple uniform of the professional working woman: tailored jacket and skirt in conservative dark hue. This lady-means-business look was in contrast to the purple and white dashiki she had worn to dinner a few nights earlier. But then and now she strode with head held high, hers a noble carriage. What had most impressed me about Pam was her forthrightness in speech and spirit. She was not quite adversarial but firmly assured of her opinions.

"Young, single, professional female" was Pam's "category," according to the typed notes that had been given to me by Bethel's attorney and member Leronia Josey. Pam, now a thirty-four-year-old attorney, was one of dozens introduced to me in this way—by name and category—when I first came to Bethel to solicit stories from among the thousands of people joining this church.

The names had been chosen from among the ten thousand members because they had somehow stood out in church activity and also because their tales of coming back to church had been either particularly memorable or entirely commonplace. They were either special or common representatives of Bethel's burgeoning congregation. Whereas Pam was a "young, single, professional woman," someone else was described as a "reformed drug addict now choir member." The "single male parent" was present, the "former Muslim turned Christian," and a host of others that would truly be a representative sampling of Bethel and the larger black American population. All were referenced by a trait or selected for the "story" in how they'd come seeking God's solace or for the "notable" contribution they might now be making.

Pam's story was twofold. In the personal sense, she had come to Bethel looking for a way to validate her existence and find social connections in her new home in Baltimore. Her story became notable because, Leronia said, she had "put off practicing law to work in a bad neighborhood." Pam was at that time director of Park Heights Street Academy, a type of magnet school in one of Baltimore's toughest "inner city" neighborhoods. She had come to Bethel in search of a place to nurse her "bruised shoulders" and offered her life in service in return.

Pam's path was not unlike that of many of us in the African-American middle class who have been wandering now nearly forty years since the Movement brought us into this, the Promised Land, and the conflicting emotions of living America's dream, of "having it all" but feeling at times as if you have nothing at all. Feeling more like a shadow, not a person, has left us feeling lost and alone. The loneliness and isolation of pulling up roots for school and career are among the costs in the rite of passage for most upwardly mobile Americans, and, in this, Pam's aches were on a par. Her story was more personal for me, however; it had a familiar face—mine. Her story was my story as well as the story of others here at Bethel. Pam admits responding "in the extreme," but don't we all fear "the vanishing"—losing sight of yourself and your goals?

Pam's feelings of alienation and isolation, despite her education and relative affluence, echo those of a generation. Ours is a kind of generational insecurity and self-doubting that has made us unable to trust who and what we are. "I looked at myself as a kind of princess," says Pam, who grew up the daughter of a soldier and a homemaker with Rockwellian American values in rural Vicksburg, Mississippi. "My mother kind of built within us a form of confidence growing up, saying you could be whatever you wanted to be, you don't have to allow things to stagnate. . . . I really viewed myself as this little princess growing up . . . the youngest daughter, Brother's little sister, Mommie's little girl, the neighborhood darling, 'most likely to succeed.' "

Lord you have assigned me my portion and my cup . . .
—Psalm 16:5

Now in our mid-thirties, Pam and I are both in the second wave of integrators. We were not among those who sat in at lunch counters and rode to freedom in the Movement. Worthy or not, we are the children of the dreamers, a generation that can barely remember not being able to dine anywhere American Express was accepted. The oldest of my generation has enjoyed enough civil freedom in the past thirty years to have become somewhat blasé. But we children of the dream are now shocked that our own children are so naive that they must sincerely ask, "Rosa who?" Ours is a rosy rags-to-riches tale of the growing African-American middle class after the seeds of integration were sowed and flowered in a Great Society. We were born not with a silver spoon but with a shiny brass one. "You can be anything you want to be" was the mantra of those princesses and princes who came of age in the sixties and seventies. We enjoyed the immediate spoils of civil rights victories and grew up in a social optimism that enveloped upwardly mobile–minded blacks. We were all cheering the complete reversal of our legal and social status after discrimination in voting, hiring, housing, and public places all became illegal in the four short years between 1964 and 1968. This sweep of legislation cleared obstacles to opportunity and reversed the fortune of millions of African Americans. As a result of access to better education and jobs, the financial and class gains by African Americans in the 1960s outpaced the gains of the previous fifty years combined and gave birth to a "new" black middle class of those like Pam and me. Between 1970 and 1989, the household income of the average black middle-class family grew by 182 percent to more than $50,000 a year.

Ours was more than paper freedom; it was a psychological and spiritual high for a generation of African Americans who felt free at last. We had never doubted our equality or our ability to perform in the majority. What we had been denied was access. And now, assisted by Affirmative Action, African Americans moved onto campuses where we'd never studied, into jobs we'd never held, and into neighborhoods where we'd never lived in pursuit of America's dream. Our cups seemed to overflow with milk and honey.

You were taught . . . to be made new in the attitude of your minds; and to put on the new self. . . .
                                                    —Ephesians 4:22–24

"Man, dem was the days," says another Bethel member, Larry Little, mocking a homey accent not suited to the restrained demeanor of a bookish engineer. The vernacular of the streets was true to his "roots in the 'hood." Larry was listed for me by Leronia as "a professional engineer" and "political activist," and his special story was that he seemed a symbol of today's "upright man." Handsome, well mannered, and nearing forty, he had recently married and become a father. Larry sees his special story as one of good fortune and being born at the right time.

As the son of a dock worker and a domestic, Larry grew up in the church a few blocks away from where Bethel sits, at

Lanvale and Druid Hill, in Upton. He is a strapping man of more than six feet, but he still has memories of being intimidated by playground thugs in his neighborhood—"a kind of rough place." He was a good student, but for most adolescent boys intelligence was not something "cool" to be showed off, so he relied on his excellence in high school sports to resist the ever-present lure of street life.

Upton was just beginning to fray at its economic edges when Larry was drafted for Vietnam—the 'hood would continue its slide into what could now be called, in shorthand, "inner city." Larry said the ghetto, the 'hood, was still in spirit a tightly knit black community. Most of our generation grew up in segregated neighborhoods where blacks of all stripes lived within hailing distance of one another. The social infrastructure in every community consisted of the church, pool hall, beauty parlor, and corner store. Upton was considered among the crème de la crème of black American communities because of its particularly glorious legacy as an enclave of upper-middle-class professionals and public servants, including the family of Supreme Court Justice Thurgood Marshall. As the times began to change, so did Upton and all communities like it around the country. Following white flight into the suburbs, aspiring and well-to-do blacks joined in their own kind of flight away from the city. Those who could uprooted from Upton and replanted themselves in Baltimore's nearest suburbs of Woodlawn and Lochearn, as whites moved even farther out, into Randallstown and Towson. Upton slowly became a place for working-class families like the Littles who saw the neighborhood as a pit stop on the road to integrated suburban splendor.

Larry's became a first-in-his-family-to-go-to-college story. The hope of his parents was that his generation would continue this pattern of upward mobility. Success would often reveal itself in packing up and moving away from streets of broken glass in Upton to the freshly seeded grass of Woodlawn.

Larry's face could be that of many who make up today's new black middle class. It was on the backs of working-class parents that my generation climbed up. Black parents could, for the first time, realize their hopes that their little Larrys could "go off to college." They could even hope that their princesses' careers would be other than teaching and social work, often the only professional paths our parents and grandparents could follow into middle-class income and status. With dreams and determination "to be somebody," African-American students pushed proudly onto college campuses. The number of us attending more than tripled, from 100,000 to 450,000, between 1960 and 1970, the first wave of mostly Affirmative Action babies. Black and proud. Pumped up. Prepared. Ready for the world.

Larry remembers that it was a time to dream even impossible dreams, and his parents simply encouraged educational excellence. "They didn't care what I did as long as I had to wear a white shirt and tie and I needed a briefcase," he recalls. "I had to carry a briefcase, even if it only had my lunch in it." He later set a Ph.D. in engineering as his fixed star—not for love of complex design but for the prestige such a title might confer. "I just knew I was going to be a BAAAD black man. Engineering was something white folks didn't expect of us."

Larry's is another familiar story of how my generation, which began with so much promise, became so lost in the Promised Land. He is another of us who lost our religion as soon as we left Mama's house.

> *If it is true that I have gone astray, my error remains my concern alone.*
>
> —Job 19:4

Leaving home—leaving the nest—is an expected rite of passage in modern life. We leave to explore new horizons and learn to establish our own lives. But for my generation—the children of the dreamers—"leaving home" meant leaving behind not only familiar family faces, but also familiar rituals, patterns, and gathering places. Leaving home has too often meant leaving a way of life. Our relationship to our old neighborhoods grew less and less organic as we began moving into academic circles and up the ladder of American success. Some of us, like Pam and me, moved far away to other cities, and some, like Larry, simply moved from the city to the suburbs, creating a new home in a new reality. Material success in the form of cash, credit, and cruise tickets was today's milk and honey, and our cups did seem to runneth over. Our migration patterns had given us plush surroundings and Chemlawn care, but our roots in traditional and cultural refuges were being pruned back.

So we children of the dreamers first began losing our religion when we left home for college. It was not malicious—we just started to hit or miss, as Larry says. "When you get your first apartment, first job, your first sex, and you're young and you think you've conquered the world . . . church just doesn't seem so important," he says. "You say, I'm having so much fun on Saturday night, I gotta sleep all day long Sunday. I wake up Sunday, I still got the alcohol in my system, girl still laying next to me. This is big fun, this is freedom. . . . I was a hittin'-and-missin' Christian. . . . You know, hit one Sunday, miss the next three, hit another later."

In the larger black community, changing lifestyles and attitudes could be seen by the increasing number of empty seats in church on Sunday. By the 1970s a pew drain was apparent to Bethel custodians when the key worship service on Sunday at 11 A.M. was barely drawing a few hundred faithfully. Some of the drop in attendance reflected members who were moving away, but it also reflected the changing values and habits of the black community. Bethel's empty pews could have been a sign of the times and the fickleness of hittin'-and-missin' Christians, but this was all taking place during a historic period of time when conventional reasoning was being questioned by everybody. Around the churches, the larger black culture was forcing change in other traditional businesses, not the least of them being barber shops and hair salons. My generation began to fancy longer hair, afros, and cornrows, as black society wrestled with its conventions, creating all sorts of need for change in how we would worship and view ourselves. At this point, churches like Bethel stood right on the fault line of the growing cultural divide.

We arrived in our academic Wonderlands to Vietnam protests, black-bereted brothers preaching Black Power, and children of the flower trying to give peace a chance. The children of the Dreamers were no less confused than our parents since by then all our prophets were dead—Malcolm, Martin, the Kennedy brothers. But at least the Dream—the key to equal opportunity—looked then like a reality. In the Bible, Moses had led the way, but even he never made it into the Promised Land. That charge was left to the next generation, and we were the next generation. As with new generations, we had new ideas, and ours seemed to have a diminishing regard for tradition and reliance on a God to grant wishes we could now achieve for ourselves, we so arrogantly thought. Was it really by faith that we had come this far?

Another Bethel member, Baltimore city councilwoman Sheila Dixon, is an example of the spirit that my generation had in its youth. Hers is a textbook case of rebellion against her strict Catholic upbringing in middle-class Baltimore once she heard the words of the black consciousness movement during her college years. Sheila's questioning of the ole-time religion echoed through my generation.

"We attended Catholic church and went through the whole Confirmation and all, and it wasn't until high school that my mother let us make the choice of whether we wanted to go or not," she recalls. "I chose not."

Sheila says her "militancy" began in high school and later as an undergrad at Towson State University in Baltimore County, where she was a freshman in the early 1970s, as she began to soak up knowledge about black history and the religions and disciplines of other cultures that were becoming popular in the larger culture—Buddhism, Islam, and yoga. "It was in college that I started to analyze everything, and I could not see the connection anymore between me and Christ," she said. "I looked around at all the ills in the world and began wondering, How could there be a God?"

Sheila renounced the pope and her mama's Lawd, and like thousands of educated African Americans she turned to the veil—she chose to praise Allah and be a devout Muslim through the Nation of Islam. "I think it was a combination of rebelling and not liking what I saw. I also went to a predominately white school at Towson State. . . . It was a combination of Islam's strong message that I liked and of wrapping my hair [in a veil]—not because of being a Muslim but because of African style. It was very African."

The pristine woman in a banker's blue suit telling this tale doesn't look the part. She is the adman's model of an Ivory-soap girl who fits this setting well—the conference room of the World Trade Center overlooking Baltimore's Inner Harbor, where she works as an international trade analyst for the State of Maryland. But at twenty-three when she was a grad student at Johns Hopkins University, Sheila was also feeling lost in the Promised Land.

They are distressed, because they had been confident;
they arrive there, only to be disappointed.

—Job 6:20

Leaving our traditional refuges, leaving home, would in some ways be the beginnings of cultural atrophy. We were growing like a fast vine, but the church was no longer the tree to which we could cling, and somehow we were getting twisted in our own splendid blooms.

As we, the upwardly mobile, began our own flight into suburban settings, it seemed that "blackness" became less and less central to our social and professional needs.

Larry admits that as a successful engineer he feels caught between two worlds: a white professional establishment and a struggling black working class. He has felt isolated as one of the few blacks in his field and frustrated and guilty when driving through poor black neighborhoods. He even believed that residents there may have resented his late-model Toyota and tailored suits. Later he simply felt relief that twenty miles and twenty years separated him from the boys in his old 'hood.

Pam Shaw had traveled to Baltimore from Mississippi only to discover that she had lost herself somewhere along the way. Larry and Sheila did not roam as far but ended up feeling just as lost. All of our generation has experienced such dislocation and migration, and all of us have found ourselves, at times, lost in the Promised Land. Of her decisions to come to Baltimore and become a lawyer, Pam could only say: "It's not like I thought it was going to be."

What good is it for a man to gain the whole world, yet forfeit his soul?

—Mark 8:36

Membership in the new black middle class remains as much a state of mind as an economic reality. Maybe because like Pam, collectively, my generation cannot find its reflection. What robs our spirits most is confusion about where we fit in. And why we continue to look for validation outside our ranks. Bold growth has not come without its price for the Children of the Dream. Success has always been a relative phenomenon in black America, however, often measured as much by what has been overcome as by what has been achieved. For black achievement inevitably remains a triumph over odds, a victory over struggle. Whether it be in overcoming the debilitating effects of racism or the accompanying destructive pathology of low self-esteem and self-hatred, black success is almost always the result of a peculiar kind of drama that gets played out first in the psyche.

"Schizoid time" is what one sociologist calls this behavioral response by African Americans to the dual reality that institutional racism is against the law but widely practiced. We live in a world where all are theoretically treated equally, but every system we encounter discriminates.

Our dreams aside, it is likely that most African Americans with the income and occupational standing to be considered middle class sooner or later comprehend that they can never become truly middle class—at least not in the ways available to white Americans.

In the corridors of academia at George Washington University Larry Little says he first learned that we still live in a separate country. "White folk let you come to their schools, but don't you expect a social life," he says. "*They* don't take you home with *them*, *they* don't invite you to *their* parties, *they* don't invite you to join *their* fraternities or sororities. *They* might say hi and talk to you in class, but after class—and now work—*they* go left and *you* go right."

It is a sad admission that even those of us who have struggled hardest are being forced to accept our accomplishments as somehow marginal. In fact, one of the long-standing jokes among black professionals is that "If you're black, you gotta be twice as good as whites just to be considered good." A feeling that we are not only disregarded but may actually be held in contempt by most whites is stirring a little backlash from us. Those of us who benefited in the early 1970s from Affirmative Action, especially in hiring, now find ourselves defending a popular notion that we are somehow inferior goods. Larry describes this quandary: "I don't care if you're a dentist, you're still a black dentist, you're a black accountant, you're a black lawyer, and I'm a black engineer."

We are starting to feel that our generation can't get no satisfaction, and that all we really want is a little respect. It is still true that in a world where having a million dollars makes you a millionaire, a black man with so much capital is simply "a nigger with a million dollars."

Today's black middle class may be larger and more successful than ever before, but the problems of the poor seem more entrenched: chronic poverty, teenage pregnancy, drugs, unemployment, illiteracy. Success is a subject that makes even the most accomplished blacks a bit uncomfortable. For a people whose history has been uniquely shaped by oppression, the idea of success carries some ambivalence and a certain degree of guilt. If our being the "middle class" means we're the bridges for the rest of the community, the bridges are falling down. To be young and black and salaried at this juncture is to walk a tightrope without a safety net. Emotionally, physically. Somewhere in the middle.

These things become more central in our consciousness as we celebrate the anniversaries of our parents' successes such as the Poor People's March on Washington that gave "I Have a Dream" a permanent replay. Derrick Jackson, columnist for the *Boston Globe* was anything but rosy: "There is no better symbol of the failure to think new thoughts during the 20th anniversary observance of the historic march on Washington. . . . After 20 years, we should have had more to offer our people than simply a memorial of a dream, especially inasmuch as the black poor of today are worse off economically than they were in 1963."

> *I am with you and will watch over you wherever you go. . . . I will not leave you until I have done what I have promised you.*
>
> —Genesis 28:15

The fear of "vanishing" is more than an emotional challenge for our integration generation. As bearers of the torch for progress—civil, social, and economic—we fear that the lights of our generation may be growing dim.

If this generation's Talented Tenth has had more advantages and successes than previous ones, it has also had to contend with the old demons of racism speaking in a new forked tongue. "Down-sizing," "glass ceilings," "retrenchment," "last hired, first fired," and "twofers" are all new terms . . . in the past twenty-five years.

Our insecurity and self-doubt has at times left us angry. This anger from a privileged class has been troubling, especially to liberal whites who've rejoiced in how we've overcome. Much of it stems from the feeling that the price of the American dream is high and we're being asked to pay with our souls. For this reason, we are turning away from our tormentors to find ourselves again. "After all of our searching, we're realizing now that we aren't the master of our universe," says Bethel member Sandra Harley Adams, president of her own firm, Sahara Public Relations, in Baltimore. "I thought a long time I was master of my universe. You realize that you aren't so great, that regardless of how well-educated you are, there's racism and sexism, even within our own community."

Nobody really wants to see going back to church as a symbol of defeat, even if we may feel personally defeated at the time. But it is in our defeated state that we seek out a place to feel comforted. It is a closing of the circle. A beacon that we finally see. A Morse code we can decipher. A common tongue. Ties that bind. Because in the real world, the best friend may be an old mirror.

THE HOMING SIGNAL

The Second Chapter

To that place, you must go . . .
—*Deuteronomy 12:5*

S ometimes I can't wait until Sunday and I have to go to church on Wednesday nights for what Mama Lewis would have called "a dose of the Holy Ghost."

When Calvin and I started going back to church, I took in the new weekly experience in this kind of neat little way—a nice ritual. I liked the idea that each visit to church was like a chance to wipe the slate clean, with no sins, no worries. It is only a few years since that I realize that I no longer *choose* to go, but often *need* to go; it is a place to which I am drawn. Church is the temple of the familiar—my filling station, where I revive my spirits.

I have learned that mine is also a familiar tale and that many are called by something they cannot explain. Of one of the hundreds of couples returning to church, I inquired: "Why would a family pack up two teenage sons and ritually drive their Mercedes-Benz into the inner city to worship at a black church?" "It's like a drum beating, and we come running to church on Sunday mornings," the young wife explained. "It's like a drum beating—we can hear it over the miles."

Just as a drum beat carries its own hidden communication, the church is emitting a signal that reminds us of home. The church's homing signal is so strong among African Americans because it tugs at our very roots. Churches like New Providence in my childhood and Bethel were the mighty oak trees in our neighborhoods, the institution with the deepest roots and widest boughs. That I would return as an adult would have made Mama Lewis proud but probably would not have surprised her much because I always heard it said at my house: "Apples don't fall too far from the tree."

In our patterns of religious life, we African Americans are like the majority of Americans born in the last half of the century who grew up in religious households, and while we have strayed, religion and church have always remained an important cultural element. National surveys show that nearly 90 percent of African Americans consider themselves "religious" and believe that religion was "very important" in their lives when they were growing up and that it is still "very important" to send children to church. "I got baptized when I was nine years old," remembers Pam Shaw—about the age I was when I sat on the Mourner's Bench ready to give my young life to Christ. We both come from a Baptist background and were taught "Don't forget where you came from," and to find yourself "a church home." "My mom's family is a very religious family. Sunday school, Easter speeches, in the church every time the church doors opened. Singing in the choir, baking cakes," says Pam. "Growing up in the church was just part of your life."

> *Teach me and I will be quiet: show me where I have been wrong.*
>
> —Job 6:24

In trying to "master her universe," Sandra Harley Adams describes a skyrocket flight from an upbringing in Augusta, Georgia, to self-employment in Baltimore as president of her own public relations firm with many corporate clients. By 1984, she was clearly living the dream, steering a growing business, sleeping in suburban splendor, driving a late-model car. Still, her spirit was losing altitude. "I was just sitting here. It was kind of a bland attitude. It was more meaningless, no purpose, you know." Hers was an ache for more to life, and for a love at home. She was like many in our generation prepared for the moment of integration, or better "opportunity," who found it came with a missing link.

Though an active church member when I met her in 1993, Sandra had been less concerned with the spirit in her early adult life, and, while she'd been raised in the church in Georgia, she was mostly "a counterfeit Christian." She had achieved the outer trappings, but it was an affair of the heart that signaled her need to go home to church—to go "home" to Bethel. "I was in so much pain after having broken up with this guy I was in love with, and I just needed relief," she explains of how a friend brought her to Bethel. "I had drifted away from the church for so long that I didn't say No, I won't go. I guess when you're desperate, you're willing to try anything." The idea of "going back to church" sounded soothing when she was heartbroken back in 1984 and needed a place to heal her wounds. "I think when you're black, when you're in pain, there are three things that you call upon: your mother, your father, and Jesus Christ."

Because the church provides the ties that bind, it is home base for many of us. "Home is the place you can go when you're whipped," Muhammad Ali said. And when like Sandra, we are wounded, our collective ache is for a home you can come to as you are without fear of being tormented.

Just as each of our ideas and feelings about "home" is unique, the concept of home is common in us all. For African Americans, church is home, the womb of our culture. When someone feels under siege, what they want and need most is the comfort of friends. Friends that have familiar faces, faces like theirs. That thing about birds flocking together. It's innate.

Hallowed spaces are the sacred spaces. A lot of us feel that church is like your favorite chair, fat and familiar, always with arms open wide. And going to worship is the time for setting it all aside, like wrapping yourself in a warm blanket.

The way Pam Shaw says her spirit feels cuddled when she sits each Sunday in Bethel's nigger heaven, comforted by smiles that have grown familiar in the years since she moved here from Mississippi.

Before she found this "church home" at Bethel, Pam had regularly sensed the homing signal guiding her through the anguish she was feeling with the stress of law school and being far from family. She had the typical excuses for ignoring it. "It was an all-day journey to church, I didn't have a car, it was just kind of difficult," Pam says. She tried something closer: "I went to Catholic services near campus, but that expression was not necessarily mine, and the Baptist service on campus was too long." Something was calling her home to Bethel. "It was becoming clear to me that it provided me with sustenance."

"Not going to church didn't work," says Pam. "Going to white churches or integrated churches, we've been losing something . . . and living in these lily white jobs, we're really disconnected and want to be connected again, but what we're choosing is to be connected to people like us. Coming to church is the most familiar thing in my life now. I can't miss two Sundays. I start slipping."

When you are in distress and all these things have happened to you, then in later days you will return to the Lord your God and obey him. For the Lord your

God is a merciful God; he will not abandon or destroy
you or forget the covenant with your forefathers, which
he confirmed to them by oath.

—Deuteronomy 4:30–31

For the lost, troubled, and confused, the church emits a powerful homing signal that appeals to the loneliness and despair in our spirits. In that way, the church is our lighthouse, and its continually searching light is a warming, comforting guide home. It feels sometimes like someone has left the porch light on for our generation of prodigal children who've been in the dark too long.

I, too, used the church as my own private heaven, a place to unwind and to dwell among those more faithful than me, to be in a temple of the familiar. Being part of a profession of nomads, my husband and I spent many Sundays in strange cities where the black church and the sisters in the amen corner were our extended family. And sometimes you really could stay for dinner. In the church's kitchen. Fried chicken. Potato salad. Soul food heaven. You could count on the same spirit, almost the same hymns, choir, and attitudes. In spirit and in truth, the black churches are watering holes for black culture, and just by their presence in the heart of the black community they signal those of us looking to anchor ourselves in the swells of blackness. If only for a day.

The church is like the comfort of our old rooms, whether you've moved across the state line or county line. If you're seeking a physical black experience, the church is the Upper Room. If you want to find out about the soul of a city's black folk, the church is where you go.

Church can be the most familiar of places, and around the country those professionals moving along the edges of black life find it a vital link to the 'hood. Drive time is not a factor, the miles don't matter because we are missing something we can't find even with our active professional and social lives. Mercifully, our lighthouses have been sturdily built and have remained on watch as black communities around them changed. So it was to the lighthouse we would have to guide our wayward ships.

Because it is a strong lighthouse, the church is still the hub for social and cultural activity in our communities and offers patches of hope—an oasis in the desert—to those of us who are lost. At the center of the church's attraction is the physical freedom it presents in this occupied land. The black church has always been under complete African-American ownership, a shining beacon for independence and respect for its leadership, as well as an opportunity for self-esteem, self-development, leadership, and relaxation. Since our integration has been only at the job level, the church is still a necessary place for birds of a feather to flock together. It is a place of such life and vitality that it stands out significantly above its buildings, creeds, rituals, and doctrines. Now we are running into the arms of the church to be apart from the world, that we might be able to better reflect on how we're living.

Comfort and familiar faces at Bethel provide some reassurance, and these were among the many reasons folks told me they liked coming home to church. To participate in ancient rituals, if you look at it in that way, is a very humbling thing. To know that when you're dead and gone, someone will still be doing this ritual. Before you and after you, some things continue. I just love that idea that the more things change, the more they remain the same. "What's so good about church, especially about church, is that you sit there and you know you're on the borderline and you watch hundreds of people come in crying and hungry and have no place to go," says Larry Little. "The church is where these people can come to keep from blowing their brains out. Churches are like hospitals for the sin-sick souls, where you can come for healing."

For others the church's lighthouse is a pillar of strength. Patricia Wright, a Bethel member now in her forties, was first attracted back to the church in graduate school at Harvard University where she says she was simply "drifting," in the same way that Councilwoman Sheila Dixon recalled as a grad student.

To many, including Sheila Dixon, the need to try church was one way of coping with a general lack of direction. "I knew something major was missing in my life, so I started looking back at the church. You know when there is something missing in your life and you need to bring things together in order for you to have better direction and move on," says Sheila.

She was still somewhere between faiths, adrift, Sheila remembers, when she started tagging along to Bethel on high holidays with a friend, trying to find the spirit. She spent a year or so visiting Bethel and struggling between the Islamic faith and Christianity when she again heard the Word of Christ.

The old folk say that if you sit in the church long enough, the sermon's bound to be the one meant for you. Sheila's sermon was entitled "From Johannesburg to Jessup," the morning message delivered by a charismatic young pastor John Bryant, that tied the local politics in Jessup, Maryland, with the apartheid in South Africa. "What drew me to Bethel was Reverend Bryant's ability to help me see the relationship between the problems and the need for us to get involved." She joined in 1979.

It was that feeling that our generation was without spiritual mores that sent my husband, Calvin, in search of a church home. His need for a spiritual framework was important. "Everything was all just really too big for me. I needed a guide, a spiritual guide," says my husband. "It occurred without thinking. I learned to come back. To look towards the Bible. For me it was instinctive. I guess instinctive. Instinctive is something that is within you. I guess it's been within me. I wasn't even paying attention when I was a child, but I guess it sorta sunk in."

Reverend Frank Madison Reid III, Bethel's current pastor, says that most of the young returnees are being beckoned by a wellspring that they can't even fathom. "Your mama knew something you didn't know—that you need more than education and a job. Your mama knew you needed Jesus. Whatever success you've got, it's because you had a mama, a grandmama, a Big Mama, or an aunt who was praying for you. They knew something about Jesus that many of us have forgotten."

"We are suffering, generationally, from a kind of existential emptiness. But are reluctant to swallow the doctrines of the church of our youth." Let go and let God, Reverend Reid advises. His perspective is not an antiseptic view from a pious perch as leader of Bethel's ten-thousand-member flock but one that comes from his own trials as a man in his mid-forties, Ivy League–educated, privileged member of the integration generation who had also felt lost in the Promised Land. Church has always been a mental health center, he says. "The resident psychologists are the pastors and the mothers and fathers of the church. Every person brings their own couch and if they listen, the answers are given without having to pay $150 an hour."

All streams flow into the sea, yet the sea is never full. To the place the streams come from, there they return again.

—Ecclesiastes 1:7

Getting back to our spiritual and cultural roots may be really reconnecting with our childhoods. Larry says he remembers the faith of his mother and that he's back to have the church help him raise his own son. "One of the values I had as a kid was the church. Mom made me go. When I was approached about breaking the law, having sex, I couldn't do it because in my upbringing I knew to do those things was wrong."

Most of us had mothers and grandmothers who were God-fearing like the Big Mama of Bethel member Patricia Wright, whose faith was enough to sustain the whole family. "Now, you've never seen anything like how this woman lived her faith. I can't even explain it. . . . It was almost like a superstition. We knew if things were really bad or if something really hurt bad, if you got to Big Mama, she'd touch you, she 'lay hands' on you, and you knew it was going to be all right."

Pat describes how religion pervaded not just her Sunday but her family's everyday life. "Big Mama would get up in the middle of the night and just roam the house, laying her hands on everybody and praying for them. It's still amazing that we are able to live in the house with somebody and not have a sense of truly how great they are in the Lord." Her hunger to join Bethel was repayment of the faith of her Big Mama. "Before she died, she said that she knew I was searching for something and that her one prayer for me was that I would commit my life to Christ. That I would find a church."

Pat was hungry for the feeling of Big Mama's church. Though she is African American with roots in Mississippi and Texas, she had grown up not really knowing much about the typical black church. As the child of a religiously conservative naval officer—"He believed in breathing in his religion and meditating"—she grew up thinking worshipping was something you did when you were home alone in the dark. The family had extended stays in the Far East on Kushu and Honshu, islands in Japan, and was exposed to Asian worship. "We would spend a lot of weekends with our Japanese friends, so we did go to Shinto shrines, to Buddhist temples, we tied prayers on the trees and all that, but as far as I was concerned this was not my religion." When they were back stateside, Patricia and her sister were steeped in Catholicism at the Sacred Heart Elementary School in Greenville, Mississippi, studying the Articles of Faith, but it was as a teenager that the sound at Big Mama's church stirred her little soul.

In college in the early 1970s, Patricia first started listening to the ministry of a young preacher who would later head Bethel, John Bryant. He was pastoring a growing church, St. Paul's, in Cambridge, that attracted a lot of people like Patricia, those he called burned out by the civil rights struggle, looking to connect to something spiritual. During one of those Sunday services, she heard the Word. "Reverend Bryant preached this sermon called 'Wrestling with Angels,'" she remembers. " 'Wrestling with Angels' was so powerful and spoke so much to me—it was sort of a sermon about making decisions and making choices, and it was about Jacob wrestling with the angel, but the big thing was for me it was a powerful turning point where I really realized I had to be committed and I had to give my life to Christ." Patricia explains the pull: "I could not believe that I was really going to walk out of that balcony and all the way down those steps and down the aisle of the church, because I am an introverted person. The next thing I knew I was down there, and it was the beginning of a whole community."

"I made a commitment to being part of a church community, and I frankly did not like it," she says. "It meant dealing with all the hypocrisies of 'the church,' but I was also put with a group of people at the time who were really seriously, seriously trying to work out their salvation and trying to work out the meaning of religion in their lives, and the experiences that we went through—I mean, the spiritual highs that we reached were at such a high level of intensity, it was really wonderful."

> *I give you this instruction in keeping with the proph-*
> *ecies . . . so that by following them you may fight the*
> *good fight, holding on to faith and good conscience.*
> *Some have rejected these and shipwrecked their faith.*
> —1 Timothy 1:18–19

Now some of those joining Bethel may not have personally grown up in God's help but have found that the word of His truth lasts throughout all generations. Among those whose personal faith was shaky was a young man who saved his own life and has been saved by grace and a mother's love through his membership at Bethel.

"My mama knew that Jesus was Y.O.H.," says the streetwise Max Taylor, "your only hope." The day that I met him, he was completely resolute that church, for him, and Bethel in particular, was Y.O.H. Now almost thirty, Max came to Bethel in 1992, a scared man, working as a bodyguard for drug dealers in gritty Baltimore. "I was never a believer, never, never, never, never. I knew Jesus Christ exists. I knew of everything He is capable of, but I never believed He felt for me," says Max. Then came a vision in the night. A vision to his mother, with whom his relations were not the best. She telephoned him to tell him of a dream she'd had. Something about his dying of gunshot wounds. "We hadn't spoken in a long, long time, and she called this night to tell me of the dream. She asked if she could pray for me, and as she said the prayer, I couldn't find myself walking through the front door. I got on my knees in my living room and stayed there all night. I said, 'Lord, if I live to see tomorrow, I'm going to turn it over to you.' " Max says he feels like he must be a witness. "I just came back. . . . I started coming back, and I'm determined to rededicate my life to Christ, and no matter what I do, I just want to do it for the glorification of Him, because I know that He is the only reason why I am allowed to stand here and tell my story."

There are a lot of folks who want to "testify" to the power of the Lord's reach, and not the least of them is one of Bethel's newest ministers, Vanda Guzman Perry. "That girl has a story to tell," is what Vanda's jacket notes said about her when she was suggested for this project. Vanda has gone 360 degrees from singing in the choir to streetwalking for food and drug money, back home to sing for the Lord once again.

Vanda can't remember when her voice didn't move people, whether she was singing about Jesus or just getting a little "R-E-S-P-E-C-T." Her earliest stage was the choir stand in Mt. Calvary Star Baptist on Milton Avenue on Baltimore's east side, where she grew up. At six she was already doing solos. By eleven, she sang lead. Life at home with her mom was improving, and they moved from Baltimore's east side to the west side—a passage many working-class blacks would make when stepping up to the middle-class enclaves forming on the west, where Jewish families were abandoning homes and heading for suburbia. In strange new environs, twelve-year-old Vanda got her first whiff of something that gave her a soul satisfaction that singing in church couldn't. "When I got to the west side, I didn't go to church anymore. We were sniffing glue first at school. It led from that to the reefer. I stuck with the reefer for years and years, and I started snorting cocaine, then graduated from that." She had her own singing group by then, the Brockingtons of Baltimore, and they were "playing a lot of gigs" and dropping acid, 'ludes, and hitting the free-base pipe.

Vanda sang in city after city, doing background and guest solos with headliners like the Stylistics and Harold Melvin and the Blue Notes, until she ended up in Hollywood with no means of supporting her twelve-year-old son and eleven-year-old daughter. Vanda's voice was still blessed, despite abuse, but her soulful style and the "Philadelphia sound" of the early seventies was out of synch with the new disco beat. "That's when drugs really took a toll on me, to escape the fact that I could not deal with that music, that music wasn't me. Aretha and Gladys, all of us took a whupping at that time with the music. Donna Summer just came out with the music."

"When I left Baltimore, it was like 'I'm leaving to be a star.' When I came back, I was in such bad shape, people didn't even recognize me. My sister kept saying to me, 'I want you to go down to this church with me.'" Her sister knew that for Vanda, Bethel might have been her only hope.

The odysseys of Max and Vanda to the altar may have been more colorful than Pam's or mine, but we all have shared the same feeling of dislocation. It was the same dislocation felt by the high-flying Sandra, a self-made entrepreneur with a list of impressive clients, who sees the back-to-church movement among her friends: "I see the movement even among my circle, just my college friends," says Sandra. "I was talking to a friend of mine who is a prosecutor—his father was a school superintendent—and he's a born-again believer. Our other classmates at Morgan

State—for example, Miss Morgan; she's also now a born-again believer." She continues running down her mental list the way we used to say, "And so-and-so got a job at IBM, or Kraft," in that sho' nuf girl kinda way. But it was not one-upmanship for worldly accomplishments; the stakes were much higher. Sandra said, "We're all being led back to the church for our own spiritual birthing."

Sociologists and theologians call a return to organized religion by those who were raised in it but strayed as "closing the circle." This passage historically happens in the black church when people reach their forties and fifties, but a recent survey of black ministers from many denominations showed that the current trend is toward closing the circle earlier, with many of their new-member ages ranging between twenty and thirty.

So into the bosom of Mother Bethels around the country, African Americans have begun to flock. Just as our fortunes were growing, so was our need to understand from whom all these blessings flowed. Larry says his feelings are validated in the company of those like Sheila, Pat, and Pam. "People are coming from all over the city. We have had more than a thousand join Bethel already this year," he says. "The black church can do two things. Teach them Afrocentric religion and to know that churches will help somebody."

Our return home to the old landmarks, to the light-houses, is being hastened as members of our generation become new parents like Larry, who still believe in the affirming power of the church to guide their children.

Concern about raising a family is one of the top two reasons many people say they are coming back to church, according to research by C. Eric Lincoln and Lawrence Mamiya, who also said of church growth that the greatest number of returnees are in their late twenties and thirties, with some coming after "settling down" and following the birth of their first child. Many among the clergy also said that when young people encounter a personal crisis or are in deep trouble, they tend to return.

The church's homing signal is felt across the divide, however, and the drum beat of the spirit is felt widely. Both are rooted in our dreams of home, a new one in the Promised Land and the one we left behind. "What keeps me and my family together is my religion. I cannot afford to miss two Sundays now, because I know that the temptations are so great out here," says Larry, who lives with his wife and son about twenty-three miles northeast of Bethel. "When you come into a county type where the trees are growing and the grass is green, you forget how you got there. When you belong to a church, you constantly see what's going on. It keeps me in contact with the problems in my community. I cannot duck them."

Sandra Harley Adams, who had come looking for the Comforter, says the church can provide for those who are children of deferred dreams. "I think a lot of people our age, the reason why we're coming back is that we've had trauma in our lives. We've had bad marriages, we've had bad careers, and, personally, it was a relational thing for me. I thought for a long time I was master of my universe, but then you find you need something real. Something authentic through the church, through your own personal relationship with God."

SOMEBODY OUGHT TO
SAY AMEN

The Third Chapter

Sing to the Lord a new song . . .
—*Psalm 96:1*

Each Thursday night for the past five weeks, a special mass choir has practiced for this special Women's Day recital. An amalgam of Bethel's three choirs is being conducted by the First Lady of the church, Sister Marlaa Hall Reid, with help from brass instruments, electric guitar, drums, piano, and organ. She is standing, her back to the audience, in the choir loft behind the pulpit where about ten robed ministers, guests, and bodyguards are gathered in a semicircle around Bethel's pastor, Reverend Frank Madison Reid III, and today's guest speaker. Elevated above the pulpit, on a balcony wrapping around three-fourths of the cavernous sanctuary, the choir sways back and forth, a wave of white and six hundred shades of purple, the color combination chosen for both this special choir and the congregants, symbolically rich in biblical overtones. Purple is a hue often associated with royalty, so to assume the color is to reign as queens on this day, while white celebrates the Light of God and the pure of heart.

In the sanctuary below this wave of white-crested purple, we are nearly two thousand, singing from our souls, with all the pew space filled and more parishioners overflowing into the foyer and onto busy Druid Hill Avenue, where services are piped through speakers into the street. It may seem at times that a carnival atmosphere hovers about Bethel's services as people jostle for limited seating, but going to Bethel is going to church in the way many of us remember—getting all dressed up and investing the whole day. If sometimes there is a bit of circus here, Bethel remains a church in the old-fashioned sense.

The cathedral is stately, grand, and traditional, commanding reverence from its visitors by striking all the familiar visual chords of holy temples—stained glass windows and mahogany pews upholstered in deep red, a choir loft elevated slightly higher than the pulpit, just beneath the elaborate pipes of the century-old organ. What is notable about Bethel's sanctuary is not what is visible, but rather what is not. Absent in all this reverential regalia are the images one expects in religious sanctuaries. There is no cross. There is no picture of Jesus. No oil rendering of a Gentle Shepherd with straight blond hair and sandaled feet. Mary is not here, nor are there pink babes in swaddling clothes lying in mangers.

The pulpit is draped at times with brightly woven strips of African kente cloth in vibrant red, gold, and green, so-called liberation colors that African Americans have taken to wearing both for the aesthetics and for the political/racial allegiance it confers to those who know. It is this same kente fabric in varying hues of red, gold, green, and royal blue that adorns the necks of many of Bethel's ministers and pulpit guests. All around me in the congregation many are outfitted in traditional African robes, women with their heads wrapped in the turban fashion worn so elegantly by the world's Winnie Mandelas, the men in kufis, a hat rightly considered "a crown" and symbolic of the royal inheritances of African peoples everywhere.

Standing now in the pulpit, Bethel's pastor since 1988, the Reverend Dr. Frank Madison Reid III, is slowly nodding his approval of the swaying sistahs around him. His arms raised heavenward, he seems to drink in their praises.

His wife, Sister Marlaa, her arms aflapping, leads wrenching, drenching melodies including "Steal Away" and "God Has Smiled on Me" as choir members are united by the white dresses and purple scarves or headwraps they wear, swaying in that "we know we bad" way.

Reverend Reid speaks slowly, with the rich undertones of his southern, educated upbringing: "My, my, my." Dragging out the "My . . . my . . . my" in that southern-preacher way of speaking he has at moments requiring humility. Stepping into the pulpit, the Reverend pauses before the popular evangelist from Detroit, Jackie McCullough, who has come to preach during the thirtieth anniversary of Bethel's Women's

Day, and leans forward toward the waiting congregation: "Somebody ought to say Amen."

This is the day that the Lord has made, let us rejoice and be glad in it.

—Psalm 118:24

As social centers in our communities, churches have long been our stages for theatre, and Bethel continues in that grand tradition. Historically, churches like Bethel have been venues of first (or last) resort for all types of African-American performers, from opera singers to drama groups to distinguished lecturers. Bethel's pulpit has held many visiting speakers in the past, including abolitionist Frederick Douglass and crusading journalist Ida B. Wells. It is often host to traveling evangelists like today's speaker.

"Let us lift up our eyes unto the hills," the evangelist intones in a small, hurrying voice. Her message is taken from the story of Jesus' trial that led to his crucifixion. Her sermon questions where Jesus had moments of self-doubt or low self-esteem in those final hours.

"All of us need affirmation. I don't care how big and bad you are," she preaches. "You need for somebody to tell you sometime that you're all right. Only an egotistical maniac thinks that everyone loves him or loves her." Her suggestion that even Jesus may have suffered from momentary doubts is intended to offer hope to the troubled and confused gathered here today. She preaches that even though some of us may have been feeling defeated, we can move beyond those feelings. Because Jesus admonishes us: "If the World hates you, remember they first hated me."

"We've been told a whole lotta things as a nation," she says to the "amens," "teach, Sistahs," and "mmmhummms" that can be heard around the church. "You know there are some people who can't stand you. Just by the way you sit. They don't like it. The way you comb your hair, they can't stand it. No reason," she preaches, to the laughter of the congregation. "You're told you're ugly and you'll never be any good. And your nose is as wide as your grandfather's, and your hair is kinky like your grandmother's. But isn't it so good to know that you can come in here and hear somebody say, 'I love you' with the love of the Lord.

"Many of us have not been hugged today. Many of us don't get hugged. Many people have never been kissed and told some positive things. We live from day to day without being cared for and caressed, and positive things are not being poured into us," she continues. "We need that affirmation. That's part of human nature. You need to go where you won't feel rejected. You need to have somebody tell you that you're the best friend that I have."

"AFFIRMATION!" she shouts toward the climax of her message.

"Hallelujah, Affirmation!"

By now half the cheering congregation is hanging on every word, and her words are softened to deliver the moral. "Turn around and tell somebody, 'I love you.' " Obedient I-love-yous echo around us.

Most of the congregation is now standing, applauding, and the musicians have chimed in to heighten the emotions. "What is the lesson this morning?" she asks. And answering her own query, "To walk out of here and do not hang your head. If Jesus healed you, declare it. He's not a spiritual Sugar Daddy, He's not just a rent payer, He will build you. He's not just a BMW giver, he will tell you who you're going to be. If you declare for Jesus, he will say positive things to you," she preaches.

"We're set up in a structure that rejects us as a people . . . that ignores our cries. The cries of our children. So we can't afford to go somewhere and have our palms read or dial 1–900–psychic. We've got to believe in the living God. That is why the church is such a powerful place," she continues. "That's why you can always come in this place and be affirmed. To know that you're not standing independent.

"Turn around and tell somebody, 'I love you.' " Again, the chorus of I-love-yous sounds.

"Hallelujah! Affirmation!"

Pam Shaw was sitting down near the front during the service and recalls being so moved that she sat with her arms wrapped around herself in a cozy bear hug, rocking slowly backward and forward in her pew. Feeling the afterglow of good preaching, anticipating more. Flashing back to before she was a woman in need of such affirming. "Girlfriend was awesome," she said, the verbal high-five for the evangelist. "Girlfriend had the place jumping."

Better is one day in your courts than a thousand elsewhere.

—Psalm 84:10

An enthusiastic worship in the tent-revival, leap-of-faith style with lots of singing and dancing around is almost a cliché—typical of rural black Baptists or backwater Pentecostals. But religion and black culture are so integrated that the symbols of the black church have come to be recognized more broadly as a "black thang" than a Jesus thang. While each denomination has its own worship style, this Bethel service would best conjure up the image most Americans have of our church services—the cookie-cutter image of rows of hefty sisters jumping, shouting, and praising "the Lawd." It is an over-simplified, narrow caricature of African-American culture, but as with all caricatures there is a glimpse of the real there. In terms of racial stereotypes, the shouting sister is right up there with watermelon, ribs, and fried chicken. It's one of those really black thangs like collard greens on Sunday. Like Amos 'n' Andy, Aunt Jemima, and Superfly—shuffling, smiling, potential gangstas, each has a kernel of somebody we know. Those are things that still make some middle-class African Americans, even some of Bethel's members, a little uneasy, a little concerned about "decorum."

It is hard to describe to the casual observer what "having church" means. I once listened to a distinguished, earnest white scholar talk about how "exotic" and stirring a worship he'd experienced in a southern black Baptist church—he said he felt like he swallowed five loaves of white bread and was full of the staff of life. Being full of the Holy Ghost *is* like feasting on the staff of life, and through music and sermons, Bethel's worship serves up soul food of a basic kind.

Getting people to sing together is a well-known device for making them comfortable and establishing a sense of community. Bethel's is a particularly snug evangelical service, with a great deal of attention paid to nurturing, exchanging hugs with pew partners, joining hands in small prayer circles, and later in the service forming a human chain with everyone around the sanctuary locking fingers. Music is the lifeblood of a soulful worship service, and Bethel's ministers of music play an important role in the theatre and the salvation of souls. Bethelites like a joyful noise. Singing is second only to preaching as a magnet for attracting new members, and it is the primary vehicle for spiritually transporting the entire congregation.

Most Sundays Bethel attracts more people than it can seat. A sin, Reverend Reid believes, that threatens to alienate both the neighbors and the congregants of Bethel, three-fourths of whom drive at least thirty minutes one way to get there. Nearly ten thousand people call Bethel their church home, and each of the three Sunday services, at 8:30 A.M., 11 A.M., and 6 P.M., attracts about fifteen hundred, a standing-room-only event each time. A surprisingly good number of Bethel members, like Patricia Wright, are what they call three-timers, which means that they attend all three worship services each Sunday, about eight hours of singing thanks and praises unto the Lord. Church is truly an all-day thing. You can go out to dinner or bring it into the large banquet hall upstairs. This time in church is not a penitence at hoe, but the taste of joy divine they've craved all week. "There are just three things that I could sit through all day," says Patricia. "Tennis matches, dance performances, and church services." In a way, Patricia believes she's making up for lost time, when she couldn't feel the spirit that this kind of African-inspired worship offers.

It was as a teenager that Patricia felt the Spirit in hearing the sounds at Big Mama's church. Big Mama's church was out in rural Mississippi—an old, speaking-in-tongues type. "I was fascinated more by the music and by the worship through the music," she says. "I had been to all kinds of services on the bases, but more than anyplace else I enjoyed the Baptist tradition."

Singing and the performance associated with it are what is called the "characteristic logo" of African-American worship style. Shouting, "holy dancing," and speaking in tongues are encouraged as signs of the spirit of Jesus at work and an acceptance of a unique African-American expression of the gospel. There are variations on the use of music depending on the religious denomination, for sure, but a strong reliance on the idea of music setting the spiritual mood can be traced to our African heritage. In the same way that our family trees can be traced to Africa, so can some of our customs and religious signatures. Spirit possession and shouting as expressions of worship are uniquely African and African American. West African peoples ritually have group experiences involving drumming and singing and clapping that lead to a kind of trance. Early black churches would practice the "ring shout," forming a circle to the cadence of a favorite shout or song, or the "running spiritual," in which members would shuffle, "jerk," and "bump" by clapping and slapping their bodies in spiritual dancing that could last up to eight hours at a time.

Much of what and how we worship in church can be traced through our cultural and historical roots. Our religious music often reflects our earthly struggles. It has been called "unity music" because it unites us in expressing our joys, sorrows, hates, loves, and hopes. Singing together in our churches is so soul-felt because it is liberating and because it affirms that being black is possible only in a communal context. What a joy divine to stand in praise of what our ancestors created, and how it revives our spirits. Since this singing and shouting in church is probably one of the "blackest" things you can do, many, many Bethel members like Patricia have struggled to overcome what Bethel teaches are "anti-African values," notions, for example, that it is wrong to be emotional or to clap your hands to the beat. Bethel's pastor describes this worship as "holistic"— the church has something for your mind, body, and soul. In West Africa, music, religion, and life are still considered a holistic experience. As Bethel's newer members have begun to embrace this kind of "new" enthusiastic worship, they are in fact revisiting the roots of our African-American religion—a trip that has reconnected many of us to our souls as well.

How right they are to adore you!

—Song of Songs 1:4

Bethel's Vanda Guzman Perry, a lay minister and frequent, beloved soloist with the church's choirs, says singing in church is mind-altering, a metaphysical experience in which she feels like a channel for the Almighty. "I feel completely like the Lord is working inside me." With her musical gifts, Vanda would remind you of the hundreds in choir stands across African America who can bend notes, wail, and falsetto anything from "Hark! the Herald" to "Ain't No Ways Tired." It's the kind of singing that inspires compliments: "Chil', that girl can sang. She tore that song *up*." We do love our divas, and testaments to Vanda's gifts overflow. My favorite is from the seasoned Bethel deaconess in proper Sunday hat and sensible shoes: "Vanda sings and people find God."

If it is music that soothes the beast within each of us, then "the beat" is at the very heart of what has been Bethel's calculated model for reviving the spirit. Bethel's is not a "pie crust religion." That's something with no filling in the middle, I read once in a slave narrative on worship: "Old-time religion had some filling between the crusts. . . . Wasn't so much empty words, like they is today . . . get some filling in their pie crust religion so's when they meet the Lord, their souls won't be empty."

We have historically relied on church worship for personal affirmation and self-esteem to compensate for emotional restraints we may have felt imposed upon us by the majority culture. Church is a needed chance to let off some steam; it plays a cathartic role. The role of the church today in African-American lives is the same as the one it was reported by scholar Kenneth B. Clark to have played in 1950: "a social and recreation club and a haven of comfort for the masses."

Bethel wants to be seen as a filling station for the soul. By design, it is a charismatic worship service. The music helps you to become physically and emotionally involved, says

Reverend Reid. "If the focus is on the beat in African-American worship services, then it's no longer an intellectual experience. It becomes an emotional experience, which is, in itself, biblical. The book says: 'Thou shall love the Lord thy God with all thy heart, with all thy soul, and with all thy mind.'"

But Bethel's spiritual evolution was also to be infused with the same "black and proud" spirit that has begun to infuse all black secular life, too. This kind of in-your-face attitude at Bethel is immediately felt, and I was drawn to this church because of it. What we'd call getting some of that ole-time religion is what we see as "authentic." Hymns like "Steal Away, Steal Away Home" invite the spirits of slave ancestors, energizing the morning's worship. Though Bethel's worship seems on its face to be committed only to contemporary music, its members have not discarded tradition and in fact have turned to embrace the past. What our returning generation seems to hunger for most is the sound of the hymns our mothers would sing on bended knees, sometimes, alone in the wee hours of the morning. The rise in membership at churches like Bethel reflects what my generation is seeking— a place where you "shout and get happy."

I kept thinking how very different Bethel's jumping worship was from the AMEs of my childhood memories. "Dry churches" we used to call 'em. Actually, there was only one. The Emmery Chapel AME in my hometown of Ashburn was dry and had relatively few members, who met only on second

Sundays. But it was attended by many influential and earnest black families, anchored by Hodge and Hattie King, by far the most respected among our black leaders in Turner County, Georgia. Being from the shouting, moaning, church-all-day-on-Sunday, Baptist tradition that we were, we thought the dignified, by-the-hymnal service of the AME rather somber and reflective of the denomination's image as socially responsible. In my worldview, Baptists were Baptists. AMEs were something else, just like the Lutherans, Pentecostals, and Catholics. Calling somebody an AME was more telling than just what church they went to. It was a character trait. Most times a good one. It usually meant they were "about doing something," but you might wanna drop a couple of No-Doz before the service.

Each Sunday at Bethel, the parking crunches, the excited jockeying for seats, and the expanding pleas for the "building fund" continue the resurrection of a church that like most of its current congregants once lost its way in the new Promised Land. That Bethel's congregation and those of other middle-class churches would now return to embrace the shouting sisters has caused great excitement and rancor and some confusion within Bethel and the larger African Methodist Episcopal denomination. The Bethel of the first half of this century would not recognize the "rocking" Bethel shaking the rafters at 1300 Druid Hill today. But then, times have had to change in the last two hundred or so years since Bethel has been on watch.

In 1975 there came a Shepherd of the Lord, one that many, many at Bethel still call "our Moses." The thirty-one-year-old Reverend Dr. John Richard Bryant, like many of the new members in his congregation a sheep who had been lost, returned to his boyhood church pledging to make it what Bethel today calls itself: "Headquarters for the Holy Ghost."

He has made us competent as ministers of a new covenant—not of the letter but of the Spirit; for the letter kills, but the Spirit gives life.

—2 Corinthians 3:6

When John Bryant returned, Bethel was pretty much as it had been since the turn of the century in the way it went about the business of worshipping the Lord. Since its founding in 1785, it had been among Baltimore's largest congregations and had always attracted the community's most prominent. By denomination bylaws and the wishes of its parishioners, Bethel had tended toward proper "decorum." Decorum could be described as a complex system of behaviors and social customs and notions of how civilized society behaved that blacks had gleaned from observing white society. Bethel was recognized as a kinda siddity church with uppity black folk, but still an important holy meeting ground in segregated America. Churches like Bethel served in prosperous black neighborhoods like Upton for decades but began to find themselves obsolete in the mid-sixties when their social and political missions seemed fulfilled with the earning of legal integration and the lessening need for segregated residential living. They became little more than white elephants in a world that was favoring a zebra's integrated hue.

Bethel's gospel seemed to lose its appeal in the late 1960s when individual and collective black identity challenged these institutions. From 1968 to 1975, Bethel was pastored by Reverend Walter L. Hilderbrand, who was a gifted biblical scholar and a strict adherent to church doctrines. Black consciousness was becoming a competing attraction, and children and their parents left the old ships of Zion. Bethel's membership continued its tailspin, from an average of two thousand in the 1960s to fewer than five hundred, becoming a shadow of itself by the time John Bryant returned home.

The one who could be called Bethel's John the Baptist was back home in his father's house, literally and figuratively. Bethel in 1975 had remained virtually unremodeled for thirty years. In structure and in spirit, it seemed a little stale to John Bryant. The empty pews he faced on his first Sundays in the old pulpit were evidence that Bethel was no longer relevant as it had been when his daddy, Harrison James Bryant, had pastored the church from 1949 until 1964, when he was named a bishop.

As the son of a bishop, John had grown up in the middle class, and Baltimore was home for his family of six children. It is a cliché of pastor's kids, but John Bryant was, by most accounts, a bad boy, which he says was "anger and low self-esteem." "The classic playground bully," remembers Bethel's George Rice, a childhood playmate of the young Bryant who has since been drawn to the ministry by his friend's teachings.

John Bryant's path was typical of those of us in the integration generation. When he left Bethel and Baltimore after earning a bachelor of arts in history at Morgan State University, he went off to Africa to join the Peace Corps, teaching in Liberia in 1965. His is a familiar story of one who wandered from "home," finding a desire to connect to something larger—something he had first found in West Africa. "In Liberia, I became myself," he recalled for a biographer. "I was no longer called the son of Harrison Bryant. I saw that black people were in charge, and I came into contact with the African tradition of worship." His baptism in the worship styles of the Motherland would later influence his ministry and impact the entire denomination.

Bryant came back to Bethel in 1975 an energetic, newly married man. He and his wife, Cecilia Bryant, herself an AME minister, were shaped by all the aspirations and frustrations of our generation. The Reverends Bryant were among a cadre of young seminarians and ministers of that time who were leading churches and encouraging worship of the "full gospel," or a style sociologists often call neo-Pentecostalism. In

many respects, Bryant was steeped in the charismatic movement that began sweeping other religious faiths as well, in
which adherents engaged in healing, prophecy, speaking in
tongues, and other mystical practices rooted in a literal
reading of the New Testament.

At the same time, the Bryants were influenced as college
students by the emergence in the 1960s of "black liberation theology," which promoted an Afrocentric perspective on the Word. Unlike many charismatic movements,
which tend to be conservative, the full-gospel preachers like
Bryant were aggressively liberal, politically and socially. Neo-
Pentecostal services contain elements of enthusiasm that are
common to black worship in general, but they are more
fervent and tend to draw on the black folk tradition, which
stresses spirit-filled experiences. One of the appeals of the
current movement is its emphasis on a deeper spirituality, the
need for a second blessing of the Holy Spirit. John Bryant says
that as the fifty-second pastor in Bethel's two hundred-year
history, all he wanted to do was to return to the roots of
African-American worship.

The appointment was good timing for both Bryant and
Bethel. Although within the politics of the AME denomination, John Bryant's appointment would be a source of angst
for those at Bethel who favored the status quo, it would be
celebrated by those who felt that reviving the spirit and the
community's interest in worship was paramount to church
politics. Reverend Bryant had earned the respect of church

elders. He had a reputation as a church builder while still in his early twenties.

His first church, Bethel AME in Fall River, Massachusetts, was an example. The church began with eight members and grew to sixty members within two years. In his preaching at the Fall River church, Bryant emphasized the spiritual identity that had been kindled within him during his time in Africa. After attending Boston University as a grad student, he earned a second appointment, to St. Paul AME Church in Cambridge, and that church also grew tremendously— from two hundred to twelve hundred members in five years.

When Bryant came back to the Baltimore Bethel, he was the youngest ever at thirty-one to pastor there. The idea of one of such a tender age leading the second-oldest AME church in the country was not comforting to some elders. While it is romantic in hindsight to think that his coming heralded a greater future for Bethel, he was welcomed with the same lukewarm reception that John the Baptist received when he first came to the desert. Like John the Baptist, Bryant was not himself the light, he came only as a witness to the light. It was not with irreverence that John Bryant set out to rebuild a church but with complete reverence to what he calls the ole-time religion.

Bryant had one formula he thought would work: Let's start jamming for Jesus. He first wanted the congregation to make some noise.

Somebody say Oh yeah!
Oh yeah!

When the Lord brought back the captives to Zion, . . .
our mouths were filled with laughter, our tongues with
songs of joy.

—Psalm 126:1–2

It was time to bring in the band, to make a joyful noise,
because it was John Bryant who would start to rebuild Bethel's
music ministry. It was John Bryant who would bring in the
drums. The obvious changes made by Bryant mirrored what
was happening in the larger life of African-American religious music. Gospel music was just taking hold in the late
sixties and early seventies when Andre Crouch, Tremaine
Hawkins, Reverend James Cleveland, and later Reverend Al
Green and Sister Shirley Caesar started what is now called a
"gospel ministry." The idea of the "performed word" was not
novel to African Americans, but this gospel music offered the
same message of salvation from suffering and was accompanied by strings, basses, and synthesized keyboards. For
Bryant, the musical ensembles, especially the drums, symbol-
ized an important connection to African culture and a re-
minder that slave masters had banned the use of drums
throughout most of the South, fearful of the unknown com-

munications they could convey. To revive the use of the drum in worship was a tangible way of reclaiming the past. The musical ensemble not only played traditional Methodist hymns and the black spirituals, but they also began to introduce the livelier, upbeat music that has helped attract young people to the church. Bethel didn't throw away its pew hymnals, but the sounds of a new song were heralding new members. To appease an older congregation growing increasingly uncomfortable with such a jazzy worship style, Bryant tread both ways, immediately steeping himself in the whole spirituality ministry—worship, preaching, Bible study, prayer meetings, and love feasts to celebrate engagements. Some were attracted by the music, others by the new-sounding message of John Bryant.

The message was simple. *We are* because *He is.* We are children of the King. We have a right to be in the universe. We have a right to self-determination. But first, repent and be saved. A new message from an old source of hope seemed tailor-made for the Affirmative Action babies who flocked to hear Bethel's ministry. "It was a special time. We were all just drifting, no moorings, no anchor, and here was this man preaching about nationalism and telling us it was okay to go ahead and be successful, not to feel like impostors," says Patricia Wright.

In handling church politics, Reverend Bryant tended to be one who "preached" his battles rather than directly confronting his challengers within the church. A typical sermon of the day might have been the one entitled "I Ain't

Gonna Shut Up," in which he pleaded for the congregation to embrace the music and Feel the Spirit of the Lord. He would critique from the pulpit: "Things in the Black Church started getting quiet a few years ago. God said, 'I don't like it— I've got to raise up some new witnesses. . . . When stewards and trustees and missionaries stop praising the Lord,' God said, 'I don't like it. . . . I'll tell you what, ain't no rock gonna cry for me.' " His sermons were noted for their emphasis on the personal relationship of each of us to God.

Larry Little remembers being among hundreds who joined because of John Bryant. "You can just sit in a church service and after the preached word and watch people get up and run to the pulpit begging for help," he says of his church home since 1978. "If you have any sense of compassion, I don't care how well you're doing, you're going to feel that, and every Sunday, every Sunday."

Many in Baltimore heard Bryant's new music. Within a year and a half, nearly eight hundred people had joined Bethel, and membership was now sixteen hundred. That number quickly doubled, and by 1978 Bethel was in need of expanding its main sanctuary. In the spiritual sense, John Bryant was saving souls. Hundreds were answering that familiar call at the end of each sermon: "Won't you come?"

So impressive were the numbers of returnees that local newspapers including the *Baltimore Sun* featured stories on church growth in which Reverend Bryant sought to explain the divine pull to Bethel: "We're seeing a return to the old

landmarks. Prayer meetings and testimony hours, the con-
cepts of conversion and salvation." Bryant said that Bethel's
new members—my generation—really wanted to return to
the roots of African worship expression.

"Just as God is a trinity, I preach that man is a trinity of
mind, body, and spirit," Bryant said. "The dilemma is that
the society here sees man only as mind and body. I maintain
that the spirit transcends the other two. And the young
people are returning to this aspect."

Bethel has come to be called "a movement church" by
scholars who study religious beliefs, and the method of
Bethel's rebirth is literally a textbook case study, "the Bethel
model." "I always maintained that the style that I have
adopted is not new, but it is a renaissance," says Bryant, "a
return to the old."

What has been will be again, what has been done will
be done again; there is nothing new under the sun.
                                        —Ecclesiastes 1:9

The "old" to which he refers is not the AMEs of our childhoods or the experience of anyone whose memory does not
exceed a century or more. He was looking to the Bethel that
can trace its history to 1785 when its founding members were
party to small prayer bands in meeting houses called Strawberry Alley and Lovely Lane.

John Bryant is a historian by profession, and his sense of our cultural genealogy was shaped by his travels in Africa and an idealistic hope, shared by our generation, for reunification of the Diaspora—the far-flung descendants of Africa.

The soul of the Bethel model is embracing God as a Living Spirit, a key to the church's and the congregants' growth and renewal. It is a looking back to ancient wisdom to find how African Americans used spiritual faith to get through more difficult times than we now face. What wisdom is contained in the ages was ours to find, but we would have to look with unflinching eyes at our reflections to see how far we'd come in the last hundred years by faith. Bethel was born in 1785 as the second-oldest church in the African Methodist Episcopal denomination, the first being "Mother Bethel" in Philadelphia. This was at a time of great unrest in Baltimore, the years following the Revolutionary War and preceding the War of 1812. The Civil War would further upset the South's social and economic systems, but blacks were gaining greater control over their spiritual lives. They were learning to sing in a strange new land. Free, freed, and migratory blacks in major East Coast cities from New York to Richmond had been extremely roused to religion during "the Great Awakening," a series of religious revivals that began in 1740 and spread across the country until the Reconstruction era ended in 1877. Historians say that it was during this period that "the truly independent black church emerged" and gradually produced a new religious tradition and expression, which was African-American Christian faith.

At first, Bethel and many of the churches that were springing up pulsed with enthusiastic worship styles. In that day, even Bethel AME was known to raise the roof a bit, with joyful singing, dancing, and praising in worship services. Among Bethel's vast archive of historical documents is a letter that attests to its spirit in that day. It is a letter to the editor of the *Baltimore Clipper*, June 17, 1840, claiming all this shouting and praising was a disturbance of the peace: "More like a corn-husk" than anything devotional, with "cries, groans, wails, laughs, measured stamping of feet." A critic wrote, "Many a harmless street stroller has been dragged off to the watch house for singing a song or bawling in the streets . . . while here are hundreds of Negroes assembled together for purpose of 'worship' making night hideous with their howls, dancing to the merry song of some double-lunged fellow, who glorifies the more his congregation yells." Could not something be done about these "rioters"?

Getting back to these roots would involve wrestling with the memories and the weight of the expression. It is only on the surface that we must wrestle with the image of the shouting sister, as she is exaggerated and perhaps denigrated by a popular culture that is interested only in a cursory understanding in the first place. If it was the shouting sister that Bethelites of old seemed to most disdain, it was precisely this that Bryant's teachings were encouraging his congregation to most embrace. For the church-bound, the shouting sister is that symbol to be shunned or embraced. Leronia Josey says that it was, at first, a difficult thing, and she was embarrassed by all the "whooping and hollering" like she'd heard growing up in the church in the late 1950s. Not that she felt confined by her neatly tailored business suits, but she was struggling with an inculcated value that shouting was really kinda silly and, probably, a show by attention-starved pretenders. "I used to think that was stupid . . . everyone shouting in church. I think that for me, it was a personal journey not to be ashamed of it. To not be ashamed of shouting if I felt it."

Bethel's worship, by design, stresses that contact with the spirit world is a very important part of the African religious worldview and a means of contact with our higher power. The strongest negative criticisms to these cultural innovations at Bethel came when Reverend Bryant introduced the musical ensembles, especially the drums.

Though the neo-Pentecostal movement has been a source of spiritual revitalization among the AMEs, producing enormous church growth and revitalized energy and enthusiasm, it has been challenged by more conservative members within the denomination. During the 44th Session of the General Conference of the AME Denomination in July 1992, in Orlando, Florida, a leading bishop, Vinton Randolph Anderson, expressed concern that "neo-Pentecostalism could be a dividing issue in African Methodism" as churches like Bethel offer up "feel-good religion" that might "lessen the missionary spirit of the church." He likened neo-Pentecostalism to a prosperity religion with a "name it and claim it" philosophy, an observation that had greeted John Bryant in his earliest days.

The Bethel model, a synthesis of the Holy Spirit, African-American culture, and progressive social programs for the goals of salvation, empowerment, liberation, and peace, is framed with the notion that the African-American community operates within a "hostile world" and must be emotionally girded to survive. But in order to survive, you must first be aware of your condition.

But what about you. . . . Who do you say I am?
—Mark 8:29

As Bethel began to grow under Reverend Bryant, the tenure of the ministry began to reverberate with the black consciousness feelings of its leaders. A convergence of nationalism and religious expression was still a novel concept in the AME denomination when Bryant first came back to Bethel with that notion in 1975. Affirmation in practice at Bethel means that teaching stresses the African presence in the Bible, raises issues of concern to the African-American experience, and takes seriously African-American history and culture. All Sunday school and Christian education literature used in

Bethel's worship is checked to make sure that black people are represented positively in the pictures.

One of Bethel's many mottoes—"Unashamedly black and unapologetically Christian"—is the spirit that greets you when you enter the cavernous sanctuary. Accepting and celebrating the symbols of African-American heritage is an underlying theme.

Increasing evidence that this church is perhaps "different" from most black and white churches is directly ahead. It is a brightly painted mural the size of a highway billboard. It is overt and bears a most political take on Christian imagery. Bethel members agreed with John Bryant's suggestion to commission a special work of art when it came time to remodel and enlarge Bethel's sanctuary. Most of them had already agreed in principle to stop kneeling before the white Jesus that had graced their sanctuary, and it was removed.

"An appropriate image"—the mural—was then commissioned as the crowning touch of their expanded new sanctuary. A thirty-by-thirty-foot mural that now graces the full rear wall of Bethel's sanctuary is a painted vision of the pilgrimage of African Americans in the United States from slavery and oppression to hope and liberation. It is a startling rainbow of colors in green, blue, lavender, red, orange, and gold, more common for theatre than theology. The blue and lavender of slavery provide the foundation for the ascending colors of red and orange up to the top, where a black child is being held up to a golden cross with a pulsating sun in the background.

Everyone in the mural moves upward, flowing toward the cross. It does not depict Jesus as a person; the cross is the symbol for Jesus. With an understanding of the power of visual imagery, Reverend Bryant used murals and Afrocentric symbols in his worship services. "The mural says immediately that this place is different. That I'm black. No accident. I've got a history of blackness. I've got a reason to celebrate God in my blackness, for my blackness."

Bryant recognized that this generation could not follow a Black Messiah in the tasks of building a Black Nation until we had found the courage to look back beyond the slave block and the slave ship without shame. John Bryant knew that most of his generation was facing the same issues of coming home to old symbols. When you grow up religious and black in America, you've grown up on your knees before a white man. An image that, if only in its symbolism of glorification of an oppressor, is strong enough to make a generation of the best-educated, best-informed African Americans wince. It is a visual cue that you are led by a white shepherd. Being faithful followers we could go along with, the white part we can't. We already feel short-changed by life; the idea of coming back to wallow in the oppressor's religion is contrary to our pan-African attitudes. Afrocentrism is our spiritual journey, and this gradual but radical change in self-identity is being felt in every corner of the larger American culture. Being true to ourselves first means stopping the imitation of others.

It is not only the old who are wise, not only the aged who understand what is right.

—Job 32:9

I used to take exception to the saying "Eleven o'clock on Sunday morning is the most segregated hour in America." The image was just too vivid. Six days a week the nation was more or less a swirl of brown and white that on Sunday separated into two tones leading into separate but equal churches. It wasn't so much that I couldn't appreciate separate, sometimes equal worlds. Growing up in south Georgia, I was accustomed to compartmentalized living. While the street I grew up on was integrated, the Akins and Guesses, who were white, lived on one side of Story Street, while the Hillmans and Adamses lived with us on the other.

Everything was cordial, of course. Mr. Akin would tip his hat to my grandma Maude as he drove by in his shiny pickup truck. And Sherry Guess and I were friendly at our recently integrated school, where we were in the same grade, but I would never visit her house, as she would never come to mine, though we lived less than a block apart. That was life every day, white and black, so it didn't seem odd that come Sunday school time, we'd head for the black side of town to New Providence Baptist on Washington Street, and Sherry and Mr. Akin would disappear and go somewhere else. Still, what I couldn't resolve, even as a little girl, was that while I was in a black church, Jesus was still a white man. A dirty-blond good shepherd. Somehow I knew that across my tiny town of Ashburn, at First Baptist and Church of God in Christ and wherever else, white folks weren't bowing to a Jesus whose hair was like wool and whose feet shone like polished bronze.

"There's a white Jesus still hanging in my mother's house today," sighs Pam Shaw. "The color of Jesus was and is still a question to all of us. I choose to affiliate with a church that has images that look like me up on the walls."

The lockhold that the European tradition seemed to have on Christianity was extremely confusing and a major turnoff to those of us growing up during the sixties and seventies. In twice-a-week Catholic masses in Baltimore, Sheila Dixon grew up accepting God as white and the pope as his messenger. "I grew up thinking that being white was real special, but we weren't," says Sheila. In Vicksburg, Mississippi, Pam grew up looking for the woolly-haired Jew who would look more like her than "ole blue eyes."

I think if we ever get to see the face of God, it'll be like that shaving commercial where the face of the guy keeps changing to show how the razor adjusts to the shape. You know, like in Michael Jackson's "Black or White" video or the pharaoh in the film *Stargate*, when we see the Almighty. His will be one face that continues changing, giving us all a chance to see our own image. I am what thou say I am. So whatever you conceive God to be, there it is.

But our image of God has been shaped by white men's eyes. Even in the motherland of Africa, another Bethelite,

Mankekolo Mahlanau-Ngcobo, a refugee from South Africa who joined in 1980, says she had trouble reconciling the man on the cross with the joy in her soul. "I was moved by the Holy Spirit, but I still had questions about the white Jesus, whether it was possible for him to enter into a black woman's heart because of the political realities of being black in South Africa."

What was confining about the ole-time religion was its symbols. We just can't get into this worshipping a white man. Not 'cause we couldn't get into Jesus being white, but because we have come to question who said he was in the first place. At that time, for them and me, to be Christian was to be white, civilized, and free. It was that same Christianity that had been instrumental in keeping slaves sedated, that same "opiate of the people" of which Karl Marx warned. Now that we're coming to accept the specialness of our own culture, we want earthly symbols befitting our new attitude. However you conceive God and the Father in your mind, how He or She appears outside of it is vital. This question of whether Jesus is black is a powerful issue in the spiritual lives of younger African Americans returning to the fold. It's not the hue that is really in question, however. Details aren't really it. It's the spirit of the thing. It's the challenging of old, force-fed notions and images. That as we have examined our sorrows, we should examine the concept of He whose face we seek.

Overcoming the "chattel thang" is one of the most visible signs of the Afrocentric movement sweeping through churches like Bethel. Most often, such changes are received and encouraged by congregations, though occasionally members are unsettled by Bethel's stance. "I walked in and saw that mural, it scared me to death," says Vivian Walker, a twenty-something office clerk at Bethel who worships at New Psalmist Baptist in Baltimore. "I didn't understand all that stuff about a black Jesus. I didn't want to hear it."

Drawing the possible connections between African ancestors and Christian faith is part of reformulating the issue of how to live in Christ and how to venerate the saints. "Going into Deep Waters" is the warning Reverend Bryant gave his congregation, a challenge to dig deep into your soul, your ancestry, for a source of strength. The acceptance of our roots allows African Americans to look at the Bible, our history, and our culture with new eyes. People begin to see the African presence in the Bible. People begin to see that the best of the black music traditions includes spirituals and traditional and contemporary gospel as well as anthems. African and African-American religious art are beginning to take the place of European-oriented religious art.

In a world that so often disparages positive African-American images, Bethel becomes a place that affirms "ebony excellence." "When I joined the church, the first thing I did was cut off all my hair," says Pam Shaw of the close-cropped haircut she lets a barber trim every other week. "It's my struggle, in order to truly appreciate your Africanness—as close to naturalness as possible—not to have it permed and never straightened."

For many like Pam, a sheared head became a common symbol of rebellion against the Eurocentric standard of beauty, and Pam sees her Nefertiti-style haircut as an affirmation of the brown Jehovah she's discovered since joining Bethel. For Pam and many other Bethelites, the first steps on the journey to self-determination begins with self-adoration. Becoming "nappy happy" and draping oneself in kente and mud cloth, the ceremonial fabrics of African kings and queens, are among the important external symbols of a religious expression that is Afrocentric rather than Eurocentric in worldview.

Since the early 1970s, Bethel has fashioned its own worship style, like its mural, to be rooted in Methodist tradition but with a pan–African-American message. "The Afrocentric nature embraces the whole person and intellectually allows people to understand that the Bible is not the soul captive of European American culture," says Reverend Reid. African songs and ceremonies have been incorporated into the liturgy, and Bethel provides reading lists and books documenting the role of blacks in the Bible.

Crowning an ebony Jesus is part of the larger Afrocentric movement of reclaiming a past, of forging a distinctive view in which Europeans no longer occupy the central and exalted position. Practicing religion is its own statement of blackness. The messengers are not only cheerleaders, but also use the idea of a lost historic greatness, lost by complacency or defeat, as something to redeem and build upon. The idea of a brown Jesus is not a new one, and, in fact, Bethelites have found inspiration in the words of one of their own former pastors and AME bishops, Henry McNeil Turner, published in 1829 in the *Voice of Missions*: "We have as much right biblically and otherwise to believe that God is a Negro, as you buckra or white people have to believe that God is a fine looking, symmetrical and ornamented white man." This is pretty much the pan-African, self-determining spirit, historically, of the African Methodist Episcopalians, who were seemingly always aware of their blackness, hence the "African" in the denomination's name since its founding.

For the major black denominations like the AME church, the black consciousness movement, then and now, is a reaffirmation and further legitimization of a historic decision of separation and independence. Pastors whom Bryant groomed in his liberation theology, like Reverend Frank Madison Reid III, who succeeded him at Bethel-Baltimore; Congressman Floyd Flake of Allen AME Church in Jamaica, New York; and pastors at Bridgestreet AME in Brooklyn, Ebenezer AME in Washington, D.C., and Ward AME in Los Angeles, are all enjoying mega growth at their churches. "The Bethel model," says its current pastor, Reverend Reid, "seeks to destroy the image of the docile, shuffling, weak, mild African-American slave."

PRODIGAL CHILDREN

The Fourth Chapter

Carry each other's burdens and in this way you will fulfill
the law of Christ.
—*Galatians 6:2*

In many ways, the tale of coming home to church for my generation parallels the parable in the Bible that Jesus tells of the prodigal child—the Lost Son.

In that parable, there was a rich man who had two sons. The younger one said to his father, "Father, give me my share of the estate." So the father divided his property between the two. Not long after that the younger son got together all that he had and set off for a distant country and there squandered his wealth in wild living. After he had spent everything, there was a famine in that country, and the younger son began to be in need. He hired himself out to a citizen of that country, who sent him to his fields to feed pigs.

After many weeks of working in the pigsty, the prodigal son became completely humbled and ashamed but so lonely that he decided: "I will set out and go back to my father and say to him, 'Father, I have sinned against heaven and against you. I am no longer worthy to be called your son; make me like one of your hired men.' "

So the prodigal son returned home, repentant, in hopes of making amends with his father, and desiring only to give back service with his own hands.

For us, the prodigal children, coming back home to church has triggered many conflicting, deeply personal emotions, not the least of them gratitude, guilt, and shame. Just as returning to the home of one's parents after a long absence would involve a period of delicate reentry and readjustment, so has the return to church—our spiritual home.

The one thing that all prodigal children share is gratitude that there is a "home" to which we can return. Church is that home, like our parents, a place where you can return. But for a generation of prodigal children, church is also a great leveler of egos and a provider of many opportunities to cry out the name of Jesus and say, "There but for the grace of God go I." Every Sunday I want to stand in the pews and shout about all the blessings I receive because the church is still the place where blessings are counted one by one. This dual desire to find a framework for expressing gratitude and a framework for giving back to the community was at the core of why Calvin and I came home to church and why many at Bethel were returning as well.

"Giving back to my community" is a phrase that resonates among the many returnees in pretty much the way "You can be anything you want to be" drove us to achieve in the sixties and seventies. It is appropriate, then, that these ideas be linked for us, as prodigal children who need to atone. "I think a lot of us are selfish. And I was selfish. I was going to church for a number of years, but I wasn't making an impact," says Sandra Harley Adams, who also is the public relations counsel for the church. "I have degrees. I could have taught somebody something, but I was just sitting there. I have mine, and I just have it. I'm not sharing it with anyone. Then you have to say to yourself, We *are* the church, you know. The church isn't this edifice that's on the corner or on this landfill. We're the church. We make up the church. And just like we made strides in life and made a difference in college, you know, we owe the same thing to the church."

Going home is never easy, the Bible story—and my generation's story—continues with the prodigal son on his way home.

The Bible says that when the prodigal son was still a long way off, his father saw him and was filled with compassion for him; he ran to his son, threw his arms around him, and kissed him. The son said to him, "Father, I have sinned against heaven and against you; I am no longer worthy to be called your son." But the father quickly ordered that the best robes be brought for the prodigal son, as well as rings for his fingers and sandals for his feet, and the father set about preparing a huge feast.

We, too, have been welcomed back despite a multitude of sins and myriad reasons for leaving home in the first place. And so it would seem at Bethel that our return has signaled for some a time for feasting and celebration. But what of the older son, the sibling of the prodigal child?

In the parable, the older son was in the fields when he heard the music, so he asked one of the servants what was going on. "Your brother has come," he replied, "and your father has killed the fattened calf because he has him back safe and sound." The older brother became angry and refused to go in. So his father went out and pleaded with him. But he answered his father, "Look! All these years I've been slaving for you and never disobeyed your orders. Yet you never gave me even a young goat so I could celebrate with my friends. But when this son of yours who has squandered your property with prostitutes comes home, you kill the fattened calf for him!"

And the father replied: "My son, you are always with me, and everything I have is yours. But we have to celebrate and be glad, because this brother of yours was dead and is alive again. He was lost and is found."

His children must make amends to the poor, and his own hands must give back his wealth.
—Job 20:10

To these churches where we prodigal children have returned, at first, the music and the feast were filling enough for all to welcome those who had been lost. Then Bethel's reunion with the Holy Ghost revived within this prodigal generation such an overflowing spirit that it soon began to spill beyond its newly sanctified walls.

"One must ask the question, 'Holy Spirit for what?' What are we going to do?" Reverend Bryant would quiz rhetorically in his sermonizing. "If all you are doing is jumping up and down in the air, speaking in other tongues, saying, 'Yea, the Spirit is with us,' this is taking the gravy and leaving the meat. The meat of the Holy Spirit is for our empowerment. It's for our liberation and development. It's for our strength as a people."

Reverend Bryant's messages pricked the ears of a generation of acquisitive, influential Bethel members of good but unfocused intentions with a core message of self-reliance and self-help. This was not an accidental result for contained within the Bethel model was also a manifesto for the rebuilding of God's Kingdom based on a ministry that created a do-for-others attitude. A return, as it were, to the original mission of the AME denomination to provide for the health, welfare, and education of its members as well as reviving their spirits. "The church has historically been our politics, our school, our economics. When we allowed the state to take over those functions, the church was weakened, the people were weakened. I believe that our economic survival, the education of our children, the politics that govern our community are too important for us to surrender. . . . If we live up to our potential, we will not only do a lot of shouting, but bring life back into our communities." His were inspired sermons of self-responsibility with the message that until you can "touch the life of the man furthest down, you are leading only the top of the tree and not affecting the roots. . . . When you can relate to the people who can only put a quarter in the collection plate in church . . . you've got a movement."

He would quote from past Bethel leaders whose sermons are kept in Bethel's historical archives, Bishop Frank Reid Jr. (father of the current pastor), for example, pleading in the 1950s for the same thing Bryant now urged: "We must feverishly and passionately return to the principles of earlier black church leaders. Chief among these principles are the ideas of self-help and community involvement." Community service had always been an element of black religious expression and one of the first written missions for Bethel, as its founders decreed in the late 1700s. In fact, when founders Absalom Jones and Richard Allen broke away from white Methodists, what they formed right away was not a new church but the Free African Society to provide socioeconomic cooperation in the form of savings, mutual aid, education of children and charity to indigent, widowed, and orphaned members. Only three years later did Richard Allen found a church in the AME denomination, first Mother Bethel in Philadelphia and then Bethel in Baltimore.

Reverend Bryant was preaching a reviving of this founding spirit. He encouraged Bethelites to think of God as a verb as well as a noun, active and dynamic. "The Spirit is given to Do," became the shorthand slogan for a popular idea of God as activity, not only deity. Reverend Bryant watched as the flocks of Bethelites grew, and with each face, he saw a person with a set of unique, marketable skills. There was always the suggestion that those skills could be used in the rebuilding of God's Kingdom, but he encouraged each person to first understand for himself: "Am I my brother's keeper?"

In his first year as pastor, Reverend Bryant revived Freedom House, a community outreach program that was then dormant at Bethel. The person behind Freedom House originally had been Dr. Lillie Mae Jackson, a leading official of the National Association for the Advancement of Colored People and the Bethel member who had established it four years earlier as a women's center. In 1975 Bethel members rehabbed a block of crumbling row houses near the church for about $1,700 and began giving out free clothes and food, the first deliberate and physical sign that Bethel's ministry would indeed move "church" beyond its walls and reclaim bits of its neighborhood for Christ. Reverend Bryant was unapologetic for his members' collective wealth and influence in city and state affairs and thought that such influence was an opportunity for God's work.

"When we started the outreach center, our goals were modest. The most money we'd ever give anybody was $20 in cash. We'd give 'em unlimited clothes and food but $20 in cash. And the people lined up like we were giving away $100 bills," says Leronia Josey, Bethel's attorney. "But $20, that you spend on lunch every day, you would see people fighting for this $20." Leronia was among the early volunteers at the Freedom House. "This woke me up complaining. I mean, I look around, and I say Lord, my little old ragged house ain't nothing. I want a new house," she recalls, sitting in the living room of her sprawling Tudor in Lochearn, an exclusive integrated enclave in Baltimore County. "Honey, when I saw that shelter I said, 'Oh, thank you, God.' " For many, the act of service becomes a healing tool between the neighborhood and the church, as well as a personal healing for the souls of the volunteers. Reverend Bryant urged Bethelites to seek a spiritual contract with God, arranging a way to pay back their successes. Sister Leronia says she began to view her skills as an attorney in a different way, as a tool that could be used for greater good. "I said to the Lord, I'll take care of your business if You take care of mine. Help me to represent You well."

Soon Freedom House was becoming known as a place not only for handouts but also for hands up. John Peters, a member of Bethel and the president of Freedom House, added a full employment (Jobs Now) program, a weekly meeting in which recruiters from utilities, banks, government agencies, and private industry could speak directly with the unemployed. Bethel's growing can-do spirit was contagious for members, remembers Vanda Guzman Perry, "It made us get up and take charge of our lives, take charge of something, to even brush off those dusty dreams we'd just laid down. To say 'I'm in the church now, I'm saved now,' is just fine," she says, but "we need to be a people that will take a stand, and churches need to be able to allow people to be more creative."

From all professions, Bethel attracted and began to utilize the skills of its members. Oprah Winfrey, at the time a local television talk show host, directed a drama group for children at the church, which she attended from 1975 until she left Baltimore for Chicago. "Bethel rejuvenated me. It is a bastion of strength, and a pillar in my life. There is a sense of family here that eases the way, no matter what you are going through. I'm blessed to have some talent to share, and Bethel is a place where I can do that," Oprah said in an early interview.

Building up community pride and increasing black assertiveness, especially among young people, are goals for many middle-class black Americans, and such an activist religion presents service as a moral issue as well, that penitence is paid for cups that runneth over. "The black middle class has an opportunity to empower the people at the bottom," says Dr. James Cone, a religious scholar who helped shape the current thinking of liberation theology. "The only justification for privilege is to use it to empower people who don't have it. Otherwise, you become part of the problem."

Larry Little wants to make sure that he does not become part of the problem. "There's a scripture in Matthew that speaks on the idea that when you get to heaven, He doesn't care how much money you made, the question you'll be asked is 'Did you help anybody?'

"And I felt, Oh Lord, you have blessed me so much, and I haven't helped anybody. And then you look around Bethel, and you see all these children who are . . . who don't have any parents, at homes who are hurting. You see all the men and women who are uneducated, no jobs, who are poor. Every

Sunday, you see hundreds of people come to this church in Baltimore, and you say, 'My God, what can I do to help?' "

Am I my brother's keeper?

—Genesis 4:9

Coming home to Bethel has been described by many as being like returning to family you see only occasionally at reunions. You can sit through a picnic with pleasantries, but then what? Just as in going home to your parents you would have to face all the pains of childhood and the separation all over again, in going home to church the old wounds of division and derision among African Americans have to be faced once again.

As African Americans scattered, so did the spirit of their communities, of course, except in the memories of mostly every black person over thirty who can recall growing up in black enclaves where everybody knew your name and your mama's.

As a neutral, common ground, the church becomes a place to deal with what some see as a rising classism that has festered by distance and destiny. What physical separation has done is expose our great class divide. While the white majority has naively narrowed all African Americans into "them," an elaborate socioeconomic caste system has long existed among blacks, based on income, job, skin color, and the degree of contact with white folk (seen as a plus). The physical separation and isolation that came with the political victories of the 1960s, when discrimination in hiring, housing, voting, and public spaces all became illegal, just made the caste system more apparent. The National Urban League's annual State of Black America data has traced the split into roughly two classes: those solidly in the middle class lumped with the middle-income working blacks, and the crisis cluster of working and dependent poor—75 percent of black America.

"You say 'middle-class church,' and the word that follows behind is 'siddity,' " a minister quipped, using a colloquialism for "snobbish."

Because Bethel has always attracted the community's most prominent African Americans, it has at times been seen as flashy, with a membership that can seem aloof. As the spiritual home to a congregation weighted heavily toward middle- and professional-class worshippers, it is and has been described as siddity. "When I joined Bethel in 1932, this here neighborhood was kinda high-class around there. They didn't let folks like me walk over there on the main streets like Druid Hill. I was po', you see, compared to them black peoples," says eighty-seven-year-old Brother Mark, who, more than fifty years ago, moved onto Monroe, one of Upton's side streets, where he lived with his wife, Lula, and worked as a mail handler.

Ever since Bethel started reviving, church officials have received complaints about the "attitudes" of some Bethel members toward those who live around the church. One such complaint was made to Reverend Bryant by an irate resident: "Your congregation members park their Mercedes on our lawns, but they don't even speak." Being denied the courtesy of a greeting is among the ultimate snubs for Southern-rooted black folk, where greeting even strangers is expected. "The least they could do is speak," indicated the importance of an outward sign that Bethelites were not the uppity folks they seemed, who came only on Sundays, and who looked down on "the less fortunate" in the inner city.

The caravans of Toyotas, Volvos, and Range Rovers coming each Sunday to Bethel initially created a sense of excitement and possibility, as Bryant's ministry attracted new followers. All that activity around what had been a dying church was energizing for a depressed neighborhood.

If it were not for Bethel's location in Baltimore's inner city, many of its members, who both live and work in suburban counties, would have no reason to come there at all. Like most large urban black churches, Bethel was an anchor in its segregated community, a neighborhood church, where most members just walked to services. Thirty years since life-transforming social and demographic changes swept upwardly mobile, suburbia-minded African Americans away from their neighborhoods and churches, those returning to worship at Bethel are in many ways squatters, sometimes unwelcome.

"I don't think it's so much that we hate each other," Larry Little says of the sometimes uneasy relations between Bethelites and their neighbors, "I think what happens is a lot of blacks' mentality, for some reason—some believe that we made it, now that we're off to these nice homes, we look down on people in the inner city. But when you get to a point where you run out there and stay out there, and never come back in, then you are creating two societies, low class and high class, and that's where the problem comes in." This is a reality that Reverend Bryant tried to curb early on, when he would teach from the pulpit, "The church is a place of worship, where we don't come and put on airs, here we don't come and show out."

A "Hi, how you?" "What's up, my man?" or a dignified nod of the head are among the greetings African Americans exchange even with black people they don't know, a culturally based social custom that some anthropologists trace to West African practices. In these days of heightened race awareness, when and where you "speak" may actually be seen as a kind of litmus test of your or someone else's blackness. Like a secret handshake, speaking can confer racial solidarity and signify that no matter who you are (that is, how successful), you haven't lost touch with your roots. This can be a double-edged situation for those in the middle class. Some black professionals go out of their way to "speak" to the brothers in the mail room but, at the same time, are awkward about "speaking" to each other in public settings.

Those who simplify the discussion believe the departure of middle- and upper-class blacks from traditional segregated urban neighborhoods into the suburbs led to the dissolution of social structures, a collapse of black businesses, school failures, family breakups, and a generation of unchurched children. And with these "structural" changes came a gradual withdrawal of middle-class blacks from streets like those surrounding Bethel. As on Druid Hill Avenue and McCulloh Street, where doctors and lawyers once lived across the street from working-class African Americans and served as role models but moved away to "integrate." This does not mean all upwardly mobile blacks have moved to the suburbs, but the social contact between members of different economic groups that was once available in cohesive black communities is not as easily made as it used to be.

But a kind of finger-pointing bothers Larry Little, too, because he's trying to reconcile his "survivor's guilt" for his good fortune to be able to live apart from poverty and crime. "I haven't found it to be 'middle-class-running-to-the-suburbs-because-we-got-money-now.' I don't see that. It's just a matter of getting out of the city, the row houses, the concrete jungle to grass and wide-open spaces. I was raised up all my life in the city. I just wanted to try something different," he says. "People are saying when you leave the 'hood, you take away the wealth and the values and a good educational system. . . . I'm just transferring the glass for the grass."

. . . and when you and your children return to the Lord your God and obey him with all your heart and with all

122

> *your soul according to everything I command you*
> *today, then the Lord your God will restore your for-*
> *tunes and have compassion on you and gather you*
> *again from all the nations where he scattered you.*
>
> —Deuteronomy 30:2–3

Reviving the strong tradition of self-help within the African-American community is a "romantic" part of reviving our churches. As revitalized pillars, they may better serve a segregated black community. In returning, our hope is that we might, as a people, recapture what we remember as a strong cultural tradition of resilience and what my Mama Maude Lewis would call a help-one-'nother spirit that was a strong part of the African-American communities of our childhoods. Churches were places where we mingled comfortably, like the tiny church in Vicksburg where Pam Shaw grew up. "When I look back on my church, there were school teachers and postmen and people who work for the government and domestics and unemployed and people on welfare—everybody seemed to get along."

We were taught a sense of helping others in church, "Do unto others as you would have them do unto you." Pam remembers that there were always two offerings collected each Sunday—a public offering for church expenses and a second "poor offering," usually coins, to be distributed to the neediest. "For me, that is always what church was about, taking care of those who were in need."

Pam believes that Reverend Bryant taught her how to look beyond her own needs. "As individual Christians we have to say that even if my family is doing okay, somebody else's family may not be doing okay. I've got to break out of this, not just my immediate family, my immediate community," says Pam. "I cannot forget about my cousins who did not go to college. And their kids who are on welfare. I need to interact, and maybe their kids will see something different. I think it's an individual responsibility that will start out of a group, and that group is going to be the church."

Sandra Harley Adams believes that Bethel is becoming the Grand Central Station of a modern-day Underground Railroad. "In the black community, if we hear that someone's in trouble, we tell other people, 'Oh girl, did you know so-and-so was just laid off,' and then you'll see people offering a table or a chair or a chance to babysit or whatever is needed," she explains. "It's that underground network that works very well. When jobs fail or relationships come apart . . . when our back is against the wall, there's always another door. If you have to move in with our aunts and uncles, we'll do that for a while, or if we have to work, I mean, there's always hope, there's always that door."

FISHERS OF MEN

The Fifth Chapter

The Spirit of the Lord will come upon you . . . and you shall
be turned into another man.
—*I Samuel 10:6*

G od seems to speak through only a few in each generation, and, if John Bryant's successful ministry at Bethel can be a witness, it seems that he is among the select anointed with a vision by which to lead His people.

Those who have been "called out" by God are often cast in our lore and myths in the role of the Good Shepherd, and Reverend Bryant is recalled at Bethel today in no less than that heroic way. The Good Shepherd is one who is kind and nurturing to the flock but is also on the watch for straying sheep and those who might harm the Lord's lambs.

Reverend Bryant's ministry for more than a decade at Bethel was like that of tending a generation of sheep, most of whom had been lost and whom he had found. His personal style and manner was quiet and nurturing, but he preached those things that empowered the individual to take "faith walks" on troubled waters. He set a mission for the church to tread into deep waters searching for ways to increase Bethel members' faith and service and ways of attracting more workers for Christ.

Reverend Bryant was Bethel's biggest cheerleader and spread enthusiastic pep talks through Bethel's newspaper, *The Spirit.* "We must launch out into the deep waters of poverty, unemployment, racism, illiteracy, faithlessness. . . . Come go with me, Bethel," he would write in his regular challenges to the congregation. "This year, we will be fishing for our 5,000th member, our 1,000th tither, and our 2,000th born-again believer. Come wade in the waters, children!"

John Bryant had become something of a prophet to many at Bethel by the time he was elected a bishop in the AME denomination in 1988. While in the hierarchy of the AME denomination his election meant that other churches could benefit from his teachings, it was a moment of fright for the congregation. The Bryants had become the soul of Bethel's revival and the spirit of the neo-Pentecostal movement, both at Bethel and in the larger theological community. Reverend Bryant had provided the congregation with the vision given him and helped lead a people who had been lost in today's wilderness to a closer communion with God. His legacy was not unlike the Bible's original Good Shepherd, Moses, who also was given a vision and led his people out of bondage and through their wandering search for the Promised Land. Without Reverend Bryant's vision, Bethel might have perished. And as with all movements that rely on a single messenger, if the messenger dies, the vision can evaporate. At Bryant's leaving, Bethel was losing its messenger, its Moses.

"After a Moses, there is always a Joshua," summarizes Reverend Bryant's successor at Bethel, Reverend Dr. Frank Madison Reid III.

In the Bible, Joshua inherited from Moses the leader's mantle and crowned himself "captain of the hosts of the Lord," pledging to be a warrior in the fight for God's kingdom on earth. Reverend Reid would bring his own battle plan for advancing the gospel at Bethel and in Baltimore.

And so the Lord told Moses: Since you are not going to cross the River Jordan . . . commission Joshua, and encourage and strengthen him, for he will lead his people across and will cause them to inherit the [Promised] land that you will see.

—Deuteronomy 3:27–28

Reverend Reid came to Bethel with a bit of reluctance, even anger, at being transferred—"in my prime," he recalls—from Los Angeles, where he was building a successful ministry at Ward African Methodist Episcopal Church, to follow in the footsteps of a modern-day Moses.

Reid was a complete believer in Bishop Bryant, having been taught in the ways of neo-Pentecostalism and served as assistant minister to him as well. In many ways, Reverend Reid's relationship with Bethel is parallel to Reverend Bryant's.

Both men had fathers who were pastors at Bethel and were later elected bishops of the denomination. Reverend Reid, in his mid-forties, is younger than Reverend Bryant by a decade or less, but both are from the generation that grew up in the church, strayed, and has now returned.

As the son and grandson of AME bishops, Reverend Reid was not a stranger to Bethel. Along with his step-brother, Baltimore Mayor Kurt L. Schmoke, he grew up middle class, the son of Frank Madison Reid Jr., who had also pastored Bethel.

The news that Reverend Reid III would be coming to fill Bethel's pulpit was encouraging. For Bethel members, his "spiritual anointing" could be assumed because he had been among the first "children of Bryant"—a growing network of hundreds of preachers who claim to have joined the clergy as a result of Bishop Bryant's teachings. Bishop Bryant has been one of the central figures in leading and influencing AME pastors and laity, and his protégés have followed the movement and are pastors of some of the largest AME churches in America.

Reverend Reid was among the handful of early protégés of Bishop Bryant, having met him during their years spent on college campuses around Cambridge. Reid was a graduate student at Harvard while Bryant was the young, hip pastor of St. Paul AME and attracting young intellectuals to his little Cambridge church.

Reid now says the battle has fallen to him to capture what has been promised God's children. If Bryant's message was about getting right with God, Reid's would have to build upon that rock. "John Bryant's job was to administer the vision," he says. "If I could get people to recognize the vision and then to really come up with a plan so that we could implement an institutional movement, then it was God's purpose for me to be in L.A. and to have to come to Baltimore after John Bryant."

And the Lord said to Joshua, Today I begin to exalt you in the eyes of all, so they may know that I am with you as I was with Moses.

—Joshua 3:7

Frank Reid had pastored six years in South Central Los Angeles' Ward AME. He had more than fifteen minutes of fame and media coverage in his successful "holy war" against gang violence, and *LA Magazine* in 1988 named him one to watch under forty. The well-publicized successes of his work recapturing the crack houses, and his own eloquent, fiery sermons made Ward a happening church and a frequent host to dignitaries like Desmond Tutu, Maxine Waters, and Jesse Jackson, as well as the home church in Hollywood.

"L.A. was built on glitz, and the ministry had to deal with that glitziness. I think it was part of a plan—more God's plan than mine—to let me taste the sweetness of the Los

Angeles lifestyle," says Reid. "This was so that when I reached maturity, when I reached a powerful stage in my ministry, I would come to know the majority of the world is not glitzy. Every day is not all sunshine, not all warm weather."

This was an important admission for Reid, that he was like many in our generation who had become a little soft, attracted by the appeal of wealth and comfortable living that came with first-class education and opportunity. But while his life as a pastor at Ward may have had its moments of celebrity, it was in the streets of L.A. that he learned what it takes to become a Good Shepherd for Christ.

Ward was like Bethel in that it was a church that was reviving in the heart of a distressed community. Reid had begun fashioning an aggressive outreach ministry in the surrounding neighborhood and to be recognized as a leader among a generation of preachers hoping to toughen the image of Christianity, recasting its appeal, in part, as a fighting religion. His work at Ward put his ministry within annoyance range of the street gang the Crips. Confrontations ensued as Ward members helped clear the area immediately around the church of open drug dealing. Such challenges helped toughen Reid's message and his attitude toward the meek—"How could the meek inherit the earth if they couldn't control violence and sadness outside their own church doors?" he pondered rhetorically. The meek didn't inherit anything—at least they didn't in South Central Los Angeles. Reid's passion and power in reaching the unchurched and in stirring the Faithful with his different, less docile spin on the Word was shaped at Ward, where membership grew from nine hundred to thirty-five hundred during his years there.

Therefore, since we have such a hope, we are very bold.
—2 Corinthians 3:12

The Bethel to which Frank Reid returned in 1988 was truly a revived, jumping place. But one thing he noticed on his first Sundays was like déjà vu to his days in Los Angeles. As the pastor of Ward AME, he had observed that while his membership was growing, it was not attracting as many men as women.

At Bethel, as in many black churches, women have outnumbered men by as much as four to one, and relatively few of the men are young. Lopsided attendance compounds itself: the more "feminized" a church becomes, the less men want to join it. The alienation of African-American men from the church is among the leading obstacles to completely reviving the church. In 1989 Bethel had about seven thousand members, 25 percent of them men. Among the first questions from Bethel's new pastor: "Adam, where are you?"

Reverend Reid says that in taking on a "tougher" image for Christianity, Bethel can get back to the Lord's work of saving souls. "Jesus said, 'I will make you fishers of men,' but either the church wasn't using the right bait or the lines weren't strong enough to bring the fish into the church."

Reverend Reid saw his new posting at Bethel as a chance for the church to do some "remedial" work in the way it approached the African-American man's presence, or rather his absence. "The word remedial taken out of context could be used to say there's something wrong with black men, but it's really that there's something wrong with the way we have treated black men in our churches."

In 1990 Reverend Reid began evolving a new tenet for the Bethel model by adding a ministry specifically tailored to attract men. If churches like Bethel have been successful in attracting women, Reid says his ministry for men looks to women to teach them.

"No matter what church you go to, whether it's Holiness, Baptist, Methodist, nine times out of ten over 50 percent of the members of that church will be African-American women. This is not news," he said. "Why are there more women?" he preached in one of his early sermons. "There is something about our women—our mothers, our sisters—and their relationship with Jesus. We must get to the root of that relationship, because if you want to build spiritual giants, we must look at the women on whose backs we stand."

Reverend Reid's sense of urgency about "balancing" the gender of Bethel's congregation is not so much a battle of the sexes as it is a part of his own roots ministry, one that looks back to the days of early Methodism when the church emphasized moral rectitude, discipline, revivalism, the study of scripture in Bible groups, and personal conversion. He believes that in the early days, when African-American men were much more involved in the church, their religious faith bolstered their commitment to families and neighborhoods. If history is to be his example, he believes that the most effective way to help reduce black male-on-male crime and to strengthen black families is to return both Adam and Eve to their spiritual roots. The sense of urgency that is growing around Reverend Reid's ministry at Bethel is a feeling shared by many churches—that black men are at such risk that intervention is essential to survival of the black family and procreation of the race.

A quick tour through many neighborhoods including Upton easily confirms that our communities are in a crisis of drugs, crime, and declining physical housing and individual hope. Among the quantifiable statistics, homicide and AIDS are the leading causes of death among young black men, and they are much more likely to lose their jobs and to go to prison than their white male counterparts. If the actual statistics don't directly impact one's life as an African-American male, the stigma of such pathos does by extension. Relentless, one-dimensional, often unflattering media images and lingering stereotypes trigger deep fear and anxiety.

In the same year that Reverend Reid joined Bethel, African-American churches of all denominations had begun to address this same issue of attracting black males back to church. "Saving the family" became the "highest priority" of the National Baptist Convention. Reverend T.J. Jemison, then president of the convention, representing 33,000 black churches, announced during its annual meeting, "We have tried other institutions, and they have failed. The church must bring the black family back to where it belongs."

Reverend Reid's outreach to men is his greatest point of departure from his mentor and predecessor at Bethel. Men are a priority at the church. He introduces them at Sunday worship services, asking them to stand, to be acknowledged, to acknowledge themselves. "Brother, I want you to go over and hug another brother," Reid says every Sunday from the pulpit. The men obediently move out of the pews, bumping knees, squeezing by sisters. All over the church men embrace in bear hugs, some comfortable doing so, some not. "Now tell that brother, 'I'm glad to see you in the house of the Lord,'" the Reverend continues leading them through an open expression of male love that has become almost a Sunday ritual. Baritone and bass murmurs sound their obedience: "Glad to see you . . . my brother . . . in the house . . . Lord."

Every Monday night, hundreds of young men file into Bethel's sanctuary for the Male Only Bible Study, a segregated service Reverend Reid introduced in early 1990 that is conducted by group leaders such as Larry Little. "We're four hundred or five hundred men on Monday nights who study the Bible related to today's issues, and we're using the Book of Exodus and stories about Moses to show the men that you don't have to be a 'beautiful figure' to be a leader. We're trying to build leadership within them." Reverend George Rice is another regular on Monday nights, and he says that the gatherings are really never about the Bible, they are really about the male social contact. "We've been studying Paul's letters for about six months now. We're still on the first one. We talk about everything but Paul's letters," George says.

. . . but with us is the Lord our God to help us and to fight our battles.

—2 Chronicles 32:8

Reverend Reid is convinced that the scripture's exacting standards of behavior will not drive men away but will attract them. Men that are empowered morally and are made responsible for themselves, he believes, gain courage and conviction. Reid lets them know he's been there, too. In preaching responsibility, the Reverend acknowledges his illegitimate son. Though he is married to Sister Marlaa Hall Reid, and has two daughters, Franshon and Faith, Reverend Reid also fathered a son out of wedlock during an earlier pastorate in Charlotte, North Carolina. His son lives with his mother but is supported financially by the Reverend.

In a place of their own with plenty of time for talking, men can wrestle with these "wrongs," he says. "There are times when menfolk just need to sit and talk among one another. I'm sure the ladies do, too."

A key part of Reverend Reid's personal outreach to men is the appeal to those who might be feeling powerless and disenfranchised. Churches like Bethel, with a growing number of men, must invariably address the two main conflicts between black men and women. The first of these is the seeming male flight from responsibility—from work, family, and marriage. The second is the rise in female financial independence that has made many black men feel superfluous.

Reverend Reid's ministry stresses using the "power" of the Holy Ghost to turn lives around. From the scripture the men are asked to look for inspiration in the verse—Acts 1:8—that promises: "And ye shall receive power after the Holy Ghost has come upon you . . . ." The stress on Holy Ghost power provides an individual with encouragement and a sense of spiritual strength that enables him or her to face the problems and possibilities of life.

Max Taylor, who was in his late twenties when he came to Bethel, says meeting with real men is part of the attraction: "It's the only time I don't feel corny holding a man's hand," says Taylor, who came to Bethel after hearing Reverend Reid on television.

Bethel's initiative is like many male-centered worship services being developed by progressive churches around the country. The first of these was an oft-copied model developed by Reverend Johnny Ray Youngblood at St. Paul Community in East New York, Brooklyn, that was outlined in Youngblood's doctoral thesis, *Conspicuous Absence and the Controversial Presence of the Black Male in the Local Church.*

A mission to recruit young men in poverty is one of the greatest challenges facing churches like Bethel, but men in Baltimore seem to be hearing Reverend Reid's new word. Male attendance began increasing immediately, and in 1995 males made up 40 percent of Bethel's ten thousand active members. Secular agencies and politicians who want to improve urban life have started taking note of Reverend Reid's work, and Reid has begun reshaping Bethel's ministry in his own image. "Men want a real man," he says. "Real men take responsibility for their actions."

"Come, follow me," Jesus said, "and I will make you fishers of men."

—Matthew 4:19, Mark 1:17

How Reverend Reid is going about reeling in these new men is itself part of the Bethel model and is being used as a textbook case study. Men who visit Bethel find an atmosphere that is kind of macho, not at all reminiscent of the churches they had abandoned.

Reverend Reid sees it as his job to be a symbol, an example for other men. If the captain is to be great, he must inspire esprit de corps to attract new troops and keep the soldiers readied for spiritual battle. Getting their attention, as he learned negotiating with the Crips in South Central, is really just a matter of respect.

On an October morning in 1990, our first meeting was in an elegant restaurant overlooking the Inner Harbor, where Reverend Reid is a regular. The Reverend was the picture of L.A. chic. I had already heard him preach myself and heard others testifying about his preaching. I expected him to be bright, attractive, and magnetic, just like we like our preachers. Substance and style.

He was dressed in ever fashionable black on black, elegantly wrapped in a leather jacket, a $500 number, from a recent visit to the Brooklyn store his friend Spike Lee uses to promote his movie wear. This jacket, the 40-Acres-and-a-Mule logo in a large patch on the back, is, like many of the Reverend's clothes, a message about black power on the move. Even his socks were a chic, African-inspired pattern, appropriately red, green, and black, a gift from his wife, Marlaa, the stylish owner of a cosmetics business.

The Reverend is cool. Hip. Def. And whatever is the current slang for "what's hap'nin'." A clotheshorse, always pulled together, salt-and-pepper hair and neatly groomed beard, he has the kind of chiseled profile that looks good in a cashmere turtleneck and blazer, a look he favors in the fall. He is a man who knows his good side: his carriage is regal, born of martial arts discipline—a black belt in Judo—and five-mile runs three times a week at 5 A.M. "It's liberating," he says.

By the time I arrived, a young man in a washer's apron had cornered the Reverend by the entrance, recognizing him from his TV ministry, nationally aired twice a week on BET, Black Entertainment Television. Clearly tickled to have his attention, the young black man, about eighteen, just wanted the Reverend to check out a gospel rap group he'd heard about.

As the leader of one of Baltimore's largest churches, a high-powered minister, cellular phone in hand, the Reverend is accustomed to public attention. After all, he is a local celebrity with a national following among those who like preaching. "Nobody calls me on Sunday between 8:30 and 9 'cause they know I'm watching Reverend Reid and they better not disturb me," says Alice Thomas, a nurse and friend of my mother-in-law who is just one of the many adoring women fans who are not Bethel members but "never miss" his shows nor the meaning in his messages. "Honey, that man's been blessed."

Dashing, exciting, and inviting, Reverend Reid is usually accompanied by one or more bodyguards, under the direction of Bethel's own security chief, Goldie Phillips, a veteran Baltimore city cop.

"He is literally mobbed. I wouldn't have believed it," says Goldie, who joined Bethel in 1990 at Reverend Reid's behest to lead a new ministry, M.M.O.G.—Mighty Men of God—Bethel's Public Safety Ministry, named for the warriors who followed King David. Bethel's Mighty Men double as bodyguards.

"Any preacher worth his preaching is gonna get threatened. Pastor Reid talks about dope dealers—I mean, he gets on it. He talks about crimes that may have occurred in the community. He just attacks the wrongs of society. Any time a preacher preaches the word as strong as Pastor Reid does, you will make the adversary angry. When the adversary gets angry, he will respond."

At public appearances, Reverend Reid and his band of bodyguards present a forceful, exaggerated show of maleness, like those wooden African statues with genital organs of distorted proportions. To attract young men like the Marriott dishwasher, who need someone to look up to, and to attract men like Goldie, who are not accustomed to subservient roles, Reverend Reid says religion has to look tough, because "real men don't usher."

A strong show of "masculinity" is a one-man campaign to bond with "da brothas." Go mano a mano. To let 'em know that he's one of them. Cool. Confused. Repentant. But still needy. "Under Pastor Reid's charge, they cannot look at Christianity as sissified," says Goldie Phillips. "If they belong to this church and they've been studying under him for any time, impossible to view it like that. The brothers who come to church, they need to be touched, I mean physically touched. They need to know that they can maintain their macho manhood, but they can be touched."

Jeff Brown, a young man in his early twenties, is among those who recently joined Bethel, attracted by the Reverend's show of bravado and at the urging of Goldie Phillips to become a Mighty Man of God.

A New York native who moved with his mom to Baltimore in 1985, Brown is a burly young man with a body by Golds Gym that he accentuates with knit-blend turtlenecks and t-shirts worn a little tight across the breast bone. Like so many of the men Goldie recruits, Jeff had gotten into trouble early, a joy ride down in Virginia with some fellas who ended up shooting up a nightclub. While he was in a detention center, Goldie convinced him to try another way. Jeff adheres to the strong regimen required of Mighty Men of God—they meet for two hours each Tuesday and Saturday for a personal inspection at which they must have freshly cut hair, be clean shaven, and have shoes shined. Mighty Men of God are not allowed to smoke or drink, so they are also checked for yellow stains on their fingers, the telltale sign of smoking.

Jeff joined Bethel and its security ministry as a personal bodyguard to the Reverend. "Reverend Reid said once, you can be content being around power or you can become powerful. Right now I'm just enjoying being around power. His power."

Goldie believes the discipline and the personal pull to protect the Reverend's important work is a powerful magnet for Jeff and others. "Working in enforcement, you can arrest hundreds of people and actually receive no gratification for it. I mean there is none, because if you're true to your feelings and true to what you see, incarceration, in my opinion, is really not a solution to the problem. I mean, that's the way society is, but I think, and I agree with Malcolm X, when he says in his book that putting a man behind bars is no solution to rehabilitation, or something of that nature," says Goldie.

Therefore put on the full armor of God, so that when the day of evil comes, you may be able to stand your ground.

—Ephesians 6:13

If Reverend Reid was to gain the respect of the brothas as a new role model in the old clothes of the clergy, he would have to work harder on his own image. New role models require a new language for ministers like Reid—you can't hit the streets speaking the King's English. "Thees and thous won't cut it out there," the Reverend says.

Reverend Reid took a cue from rappers like Chuck D. with Public Enemy and KRS-One with Boogie Down Productions, credited with resurrecting the ideas of Malcolm X in their lyrics in the 1980s and bringing his message to a whole new generation of black youth. At the same time, Ice Cube's lyrics taunted him, when he said there's no longer a need for "Reverend Pigfeet," a pejorative for ministers who grow fat off their congregations while encouraging a heavenly, not an earthly, salvation. Spike Lee's biographical film about Malcolm X and the Nation of Islam added fuel to Reverend Reid's sense that a more "aggressive" religion was the only thing that would attract today's black male.

The church's competition for the attention of the black male was not happening in a vacuum. The greatest competition for the religious lives of African-American males is currently from Islam, which is considered by some the more viable religious alternative to black Christian churches, with the main appeals of Islam being the legacy of Malcolm X and the macho image.

Islam's Qur'an advocates self-defense, while the Christian Bible counsels turning the other cheek, and the lex talionis—an eye for an eye or a life for a life—has a more persuasive appeal to today's youth and to the oppressed whose cheeks are stinging from inordinate abuse.

Reverend Reid grew up when the competing and equally compelling words of Martin Luther King and Malcolm X shaped a generation's self-identity. "I remember being in Washington with my daddy at the March on Washington in 1963, but I can also remember being in college and having the trial of Bobby Seale, the Black Panther, going on in the next town," he says.

At Bethel and other black churches, pastors have learned that a fiery blend of Islam, the Bible, black nationalism, racial chauvinism, military-style discipline, and bootstrap economics is a message black males seem to want to hear. Malcolm X and Martin Luther King Jr. have become flip sides of a new spin on African-American religious rhetoric. "Malcolm X's challenge to the black church was Do the right thing. It's not either Martin or Malcolm. It is, in fact, we need both of them," Reid says.

Bethel is raising a new race of what Reverend Reid describes as African-American Christian Nationalists—his name for the components of his ministry that espouse Christian doctrine combined with the ideals of sixties nationalism and self-help for black people.

Nationalism as they see it at Bethel is not the narrow, anti-white or separatist nationalism like the Black Power movement but is tied more to the roots of nationalism inspired by Marcus Garvey. Garvey's ideology of nationalism was one that was embraced by some Bethel members seventy-five years ago during its heyday. Garvey's Universal Negro Improvement Association was among the sources Reverend Reid turned to to find a model by which a congregation proud of itself and its heritage could work harder for the building of God's kingdom.

Bethel's pulpit has historically been a bully pulpit for the radical orators of their day, as far back as the 1800s, when

Frederick Douglass, the great abolitionist born on Maryland's Eastern Shore, was a regular speaker, as were Marcus Garvey and Ida B. Wells. But Reverend Reid's male ministry and secular approach to church building has brought one of the day's more controversial speakers to help him: Minister Louis Farrakhan, leader of the Nation of Islam. While Reverend Reid disagrees with Minister Farrakhan's theology and avocation of racial separation, he believes that as ministers to black America he and Farrakhan share common goals.

Reverend Reid and Minister Farrakhan worked together first in the 1980s in the neighborhoods of South Central Los Angeles and later with Bethel's own Mighty Men of God, who have been trained by Farrakhan's Fruit of Islam, the Nation's bodyguards.

Goldie Phillips says that the Nation's tactics for training its men instill discipline and self-respect. "I have always wondered, as a police officer, how the brothers could be so disciplined. At least outwardly, but I've learned from them you have to be transformed within before you can be reformed for society."

The nationalist tendency would be to mistrust white society and to celebrate political liberation movements around the world, especially in Africa. But Reverend Reid and others have adopted the best of the teachings of Elijah Muhammad, the founder of the Nation of Islam and a mentor to both Malcolm X and Louis Farrakhan, who was legendary among blacks as a proponent of traditional values, an opponent of drugs and alcohol, a nurturer of ghetto small businesses, and a savior of habitual criminals, prostitutes, and other hard-core members of the underclass.

The line between Islam and Christianity has blurred at times, and both have found comfort in the pulpit at Bethel. Goldie believes that in Islam, like Christianity, adherents have to become selfless servers of the messenger of their faith. To accomplish this, many who convert to Islam replace their family names with the letter X, to symbolize a blank, something that has been lost or is unknown. "If I give up the name Phillips, I've given up a whole lot, I've become an X. When the brothers give up their names and adopt the X, they have had a psychological transformation," says Goldie. "Once they've given up their name, that's a transformation. Now we can get into the spiritual part of it."

Goldie says the one thing that Reverend Reid stresses is a fine balance between being disciplined soldiers of the cross and vigilantes. He stresses the concept of "tough love," that enforcement doesn't always mean overpowering someone.

Through the marriage of the Bible and the Qur'an, Goldie says, he understands better how to marry his natural, skeptical tough training with the softer touch needed for spiritual soldiering. "I was a narcotics sergeant, and I was very enforcement oriented. Most of the people in the Bible you read about were bad prior to being saved. Some of them were murderers. Look how many people were incarcerated in the Bible."

But within Bethel, as within any institution, change is always met with some type of resistance, and Goldie says some members viewed his security team as "police." Security is not police, but to those who ask Why have police in the church, Goldie says he points out that the M.M.O.G. operate with only a Bible verse as shield: "Matthew 16:25—For whoever wants to save his life will lose it, but whoever loses his life for my sake will find it."

"That says that a man has to be willing to die for Jesus," says Goldie. "And so, you have to be willing to die for what you believe in pertaining to the Lord Jesus Christ. This is the first thing I mention in class. That's the first thing that I talk about in this security ministry."

Goldie now says that he understands that the Christian uniform is slightly different. "In a manner that reflects the walk of Christ or the word of Christ, you can affect more people in that uniform in a positive manner than a negative manner. Okay? So the uniform and the badge is a very powerful sign of authority; however, the authority that it reflects, if used properly, can be a wonderful ministry within the community.

"I used to refer to the drug dealer as our enemy. Pastor tReid has taught me that it's not the drug dealer that you dislike, it's the spirit of the drug dealer. He's taught me that the drug dealer is a victim also. He's a victim of Satan, all right? So along with my security council, there's also a spirit of ministry that we must portray to the brothers, not just accuse them, okay, but help them. So we help them through our actions.

"You can't use society as your guide. You've got to use the Bible as your guide. And so that's what I've learned how to do."

So God created man in his own image, in the image of God he created him; male and female he created them.
—Genesis 1:27

Traditionally in the black church, the pulpit has been viewed as "men's space" and the pew as "women's place," and this division follows the patriarchal view that the public sphere is male space and the private sphere is female space. Just as in Judaism and Islam, Christian churches like Bethel have been affected by this sexual division of public and private. Reverend Reid's ministry that emphasized male participation seemed to open up the gender discussion at Bethel.

The stories and lives of strong women pepper Bethel's history, including those of such women as Frances (Fannie) Jackson Coppin, the wife of Reverend Levi Coppin, who pastored Bethel from 1881 to 1883. Frances Coppin was an accomplished educator who worked with poor black people and the person for whom Coppin State College in Baltimore is named. The AME church began ordaining women as elders in 1948. Today there are an estimated five to six hundred women elders in the denomination. At Bethel nearly half the ministerial staff of twenty-four are women, as are many of the trustees. Technically, women are eligible to hold any office at the local church, district, annual conference, and national levels. In recent years, they have increasingly moved beyond the traditional women's organizations to become trustees and stewards, offices traditionally held by males. While women serve on all levels of the AME denomination's hierarchy, in terms of church leadership, black women find that the longest step is the one up from associate, assistant, or whatever titles they hold in churches most often governed by men. And they still tend to view their power within the scope of how much service they owe to the men of the church.

Since 1990, when Reverend Reid began to shift his ministry toward attracting and girding black men, in particular, like many black churches Bethel suffered a public relations problem. Some women members, like Pam Shaw, began to feel a little alienated and diminished. Reverend Reid, for better or worse, believes in the duality of gender. And the importance of undergirding what he sees as men "who have become soft" or "have fallen asleep." He enlists the women's support but is not hampered if it is not forthcoming.

This male focus is sometimes nauseating to Pam, who feels that women's role in and historical importance to the church may be getting shortchanged. "I don't buy into that 'man-as-head-of-household.' I hear this thing about a conspiracy against them. I hear that they're endangered, I'm not discounting that the brothers don't have it hard, but I've got it hard, too. I felt like it was a put down."

Some women at Bethel are worried about the sexist overtones and fear what is being called "narrow nationalism" by Angela Y. Davis, an activist in the 'sixties: "As enthusiastic as we might be about the capacity of hip-hop culture to encourage oppositional consciousness among today's young people, it sometimes advocates a nationalism with such strong misogynist overtones that it militates against the very revolutionary practice it appears to promote."

Generally, male mentoring is applauded and endorsed by pastors and church members, but some were a bit wary of the sexist overtones, particularly when Reverend Reid introduced segregated prayer and Bible study.

"We pitched a fit. We said it's sexist, it's taking us backward, we need more dialogue not less, on and on," remembers Leronia Josey. "Pastor tried to explain that some things men need to discuss and they don't need women around. There's a lot of posturing that goes on, you know, when men and women get together, and so in order to get rid of some of that, to get down to an affirming message for men, it had to be for men only. You have to relate to men differently. You have to organize men differently."

Bethel women, for the most part, support the spirit of the male-focused ministry. "We need more men in the church in order for the church to grow and attract more men to the church," says member Sandra Harley Adams. "Men are led by men."

ONWARD CHRISTIAN SOLDIERS

The Sixth Chapter

So Joshua ordered the officers: Go through the camp and
tell the people, "Get your supplies ready."
—*Joshua 1:10–11*

B ethel's Mighty Men look impressive as they parade around, sometimes in lock step, always in pairs, wearing dark suits, white shirts, spit-shined shoes, charged with keeping order, helping direct traffic—but mainly they are symbols of hope, Gladiators for God, peace keepers in the inner-city neighborhood the church serves. A primarily working-class neighborhood now in West Baltimore, Upton is one of aging row houses and the scarring of the underemployment, drug, and gun culture. Each one who is successfully plucked from this poverty and outfitted as a Mighty Man is a direct result of the Bethel model in practice, according to Reverend Reid's reading.

The kind of activist religion that is growing at Bethel and other large urban churches presents service to the community as a moral issue equal to that of abiding by God's word. In this, Bethel is reviving another key role of the church, as the place where the black middle class has an opportunity to empower the people at the bottom, with many starting to feel that the only real advantage of privilege is in using it to empower people who don't have it. By reaching beyond Bethel's traditional core of middle-class members, Reverend Reid is leading Bethel to a more fulfilling communion with the neighborhood and giving it an opportunity to again stand as the bridge between differing socio-economic groups. It is because Bethel "dares to be different for Christ" that has everybody so upset, says Reverend Reid. He says the Mighty Men of God are part of the groundwork for a spiritual, cultural, economic, and political revival in the community.

Reverend Reid's Mighty Men are the symbols and substance of the important changes taking place in the neighborhoods surrounding the nation's Bethels. The Mighty Men are part of a "quiet revolution" that is changing not only the religious habits of millions of Americans but also the way churches go about recruiting members and serving their communities. Reestablishing community pride and increasing black assertiveness, especially among young people, are goals for many middle-class black Americans. If the children are our future, our survival depends on how well we teach them to fend for themselves. Most of the pressing issues for black churches, black families, and the black community stem from the sector of the population still mired in poverty, what sociologists call the "underclass" and some in the church community might call the "unreachables," as does Reverend Reid—the poor black families that make up one-third of all our households.

The Mighty Men represent yet another layer too of Bethel's social "outreach" ministries that all have their roots in Freedom House. The work that was begun at Freedom House continues, with more than fifty thousand people being served each year through various operations housed in many sprawling buildings around the main sanctuary. There are so many ministries that a full-time secretary schedules meetings and oversees the physical operations of running social service programs seven days a week, including a soup kitchen, open food pantry, community clothes closet, HIV/AIDS education programs, teen parenting prevention program, and adoption services. As Bethel has grown in membership, it has also grown in stewardship. It has been a million-dollar church since 1983, that being the first year the trustees "handled" more than $1 million, generated by what were five thousand members at the time. The ministries devoted to education are another, more visible part of the community Bethel is rebuilding. Housed in one of the many buildings that Bethel has reclaimed from the surrounding neighborhood is the Bethel Christian School, a source of pride for parents whose children attend grades kindergarten through fifth there. Each Saturday, Bethel's "Saturday" School, staffed by volunteers from the congregation, provides additional study help and Christian teachings. For older students, Bethel's scholarship fund—named for Daniel Payne, a long-time advocate of education within the denomination—distributed more than $30,000 annually in book scholarships to Bethel members graduating from high school.

Bethel receives more than five thousand requests for audio and video tapes of its sermons, emanating from viewers of its "Outreach of Love" broadcast shown on Black Entertainment Television and televised in 123 countries via the Armed Forces Radio and Television Service Broadcast Center, reaching nearly two million viewers each week.

Bethel's drama and public relations "ministries" have revived their roles as active supporters of the local and national arts communities. Bethel's sanctuary is a frequent stop of authors and lecturers, as well as national leaders.

> *Do I have any power to help myself now that success has been driven from me?*
>
> —Job 6:13

But the Bethel model, while embracing a spirited economic warfare for the liberation of God's children, has not dismissed the historical sociopolitical role of the church. In forging a new mission for the church, both Bryant and Reid have brought Bethel's mission back to its traditional roots, and in this, Bethel has revived its role as a leader in political activism. It was the political spirit of Bethel's community activism that revived first, perhaps because it is familiar turf to churches like Bethel. African Americans, for better or worse, have been most inspired to change when led by a dynamic leader like Martin Luther King Jr.

Jesse Jackson was the one for the eighties. In cities like Baltimore, where black populations exceed 50 percent, Jesse's campaign galvanized communities like nothing had in the last twenty years. "What Jesse has done was to get people to believe that they could achieve political and economic power," says Larry Little, who first joined Bethel in order to revive the church's political steering committee at the urging of John Bryant. "People started learning how to put on grassroots campaigns, we learned how to get out the vote." With Bethel AME as backbone, many of Baltimore's 986 black churches lined up support and community rallies in scenes reminiscent of the sixties' civil rights marches. Even though Jesse's campaigns were unsuccessful, the enduring benefits of reawakened interest in the political process helped to bring about a batch of new politicians who were different from the old machine, pork-barrel types.

Bethel and other churches stress the continued role of black churches in the political process, and their history of reaching the community is undisputed. "It's one of the most important places to get people to register, particularly at Bethel, where you've got seven thousand or more bodies walking through that door," says Larry Little. "Everyone in the city of Baltimore and the state who is running for office has to come to Bethel."

Bethel has revived the role the black church has long played as a breeding ground for politicians and a traditional groomer of African-American leaders. Sheila Dixon felt the urge to run for Baltimore's City Council and won. To support political activities at Bethel, Sheila, Larry, and others revived the Henry McNeil Turner Society, named for one of Bethel's earliest pastors and community activists, which became Bethel's PAC and organizing arm.

"All the politicians or those who want to be politicians have to come to Bethel," says Sandra Adams, who as a public relations executive has advised campaigners on the importance of church activism.

Still, as the challenges of the church become more secular—led by both the congregation's desires and the pressing ills just outside the doors—traditional strategies seem to need help. Bethel members believe the Lord's worker may be better equipped than the politicians'. The church, which spawned the political careers of so many African-American politicians, is evolving to include the old-style protest that embraces placards and a new-style ministry that would be more about carrying the Christian mission into the mean streets.

In the past thirty years the shifts in black economic status have been accompanied by growth in political power. The number of black elected officials has gone from a little more than one hundred in 1960 to more than eight thousand, but the rising tide of black politicos has not lifted the boats of all black Americans. And as the black church has been crucial to each stage of African-American progress, churches like Bethel are seeking a way to fuel the new fight for economic rights.

As had happened with civil rights in the fifties and sixties, in the seventies and eighties church leaders, including Andrew Young and then Congressman from Pennsylvania William Gray, exemplified rising black political empowerment. But as we move toward the twenty-first century, it is economic empowerment that African Americans feel we must stress. "We've been singing the same song for twenty years," says Larry Little. "We've got to forget about this twenty years of racism and twenty years of white man this and white man that. We've got to the point now that the only people that's going to save us is us."

But Joshua commanded the people: "Do not give a war cry, do not raise your voices, do not say a word until the day I tell you to shout. Then shout!"

—Joshua 6:10

Just as the pulpit has been a command center to lead political change, a new generation is using the church as a war room to plan a new movement for economic inclusion. The chance not just to sit in the restaurant but to own it. Pastors of churches, large and small, urban and rural, are calling their members to battle stations. This is not a drill.

"We're in a war, people are losing their jobs, things aren't getting better, there's still a large pregnancy rate, high dropout rate in our communities. Where's the money gonna come from?" asks Sandra Harley Adams.

In American society, where economic values are both primary and predominant, these values determine social relations and status, and most research, scholarly and anecdotal, suggests that the most severe forms of discrimination against black people have been economic. An absence of economic clout has and will keep us second-, even third-class U.S. citizens. It has become evident that African Americans will have to simply stand for themselves, and the black church, with all of its economic power, can help facilitate that by creating businesses, religious scholars say. "Who is going to redevelop black America when government is drying up and industry is leaving? I say the black church," says the Reverend Charles G. Adams, pastor of Hartford Memorial Baptist Church and former president of the 2.5 million–member Progressive National Baptist Convention. "We have to reach out and fulfill human needs, solve human problems, and create human opportunities. We just can't sing and pray and get happy and go home."

Churches like Bethel often find that they are the best continuing, organized entity in the black community for the acquisition and redevelopment of land, the building of business enterprises, and the employment of people. This has called for a revolution in church strategy, and today the challenge for the black church is to move the oppressed community from survival to holistic liberation, says Reverend Reid. This is not a social gospel but the social implications of the gospel. Throughout history, the role of the black church has had to change as the needs of the community have changed. "Even though if you look at what churches were doing in terms of being there and providing opportunities for people, they really weren't doing it with liberation theology in mind," says Patricia Wright, "what was important to me is that you could combine providing the services with helping pull people up, pulling in the tradition of the old and moving to the new." Many churches like Bethel are trying to blend the old and the new. The coming-to-church-for-personal-salvation-only days are over. Now we are looking not only for personal salvation but social salvation. So-called authentic churches like Bethel are working to stabilize communities by working with substance abusers, mentoring youth, reuniting families, bridging the gap between black males and females, proclaiming a gospel of holy esteem that spills over into a healthy self-esteem, enabling people to think of economic development while at the same time avoiding greed by putting community interests first.

African-American communities have done a great deal of "soft" development—day care, soup kitchens, and counseling—and in providing these basic human needs Bethel's ministries have excelled. Bethel members are consistently able to meet the needs of twenty thousand people a year with food, shelter, education, and prison and teen ministries. Bethel has started moving into the lending business and has developed a credit union, which under the leadership of Leonides Fowlkes has grown to nearly $1 million in deposits.

From the pulpit, Reverend Reid preaches a message of empowerment and a sense of urgency for the church to become more innovative in its economic ministries, so that the church may ultimately become an employer of some of its own members as well.

"There's a young boy out here who I love and I know he loves me, and I cannot get him out the dope world for all the tea in China," the Reverend said one Sunday of one of the hundreds of youths he approaches in Bethel's neighborhood to shoot the breeze to find out "what's hap'nin'."

"Because I can't get him a job paying good money. If I could not only witness to him—and he's torn between the love I've shown him as a person, and a person he loves and respects, and the streets that puts money in his pockets. But if I could take him and say, 'We've got a business over here, and we're going to pay you $500 a week,' then we'd have that young man," he said.

It is not just a hope of paying a higher salary than drug dealers that motivates Reverend Reid and Bethel members but the idea of using economic incentives to redirect the intelligence of such young men toward more fruitful labor.

"Anytime a kid of twenty-four can make $40,000 a year standing on the corner and these so-called drug kingpins are running million-dollar operations—it takes a mind to do those kinds of things, although it's illegal," says Larry. "It takes a good mind to handle that kind of money. But who in corporate America is going to offer them those positions handling millions? If you're coming out of high school and think you're not going to achieve that, you think, 'I can't go anywhere but the corner.'"

Because of its location and mission of salvation, the church is perhaps best equipped to address the social needs of the community that it knows so intimately. Unlike traditional civil rights organizations, the church does not depend on white corporate money or government dollars to survive; the black church is funded solely by the black community. Therefore, he who pays the piper at least gets to select some of the tunes. So it is from congregations like Bethel that God's new kingdom will come.

REVELATIONS

An Epilogue

The bricks have fallen down, but we will rebuild with
dressed stone. . .
—*Isaiah 9:10*

I leaned over the balcony for a better view of those fifty or sixty that had come here to New Shiloh Baptist Church to "get religion."

They were, by their own confession, a motley crew of sinners who needed to be washed clean. Each of them had come wrapped in white sheets and with a heart pledged to take up the cross to follow Christ.

I did not know any one of them personally, but my heart was joyful with each washing and each time the reverend standing in the baptismal pool—the River Jordan—intoned: "In the name of the Father, Son, and Holy Ghost . . . I now baptize you."

The pool of the New Shiloh Baptist Church in Baltimore was far more modern and grand than that of the tiny Shiloh in New York where my husband Calvin had been washed clean.

About four years had passed between my husband's baptism—the act that brought me back to church—and this day when I had come to watch a mass baptism. I had understood

169

why my heart fluttered at his rebirth—it was the intimacy of the ritual. But my heart fluttered as much for these whom I knew not. My heart was overjoyed by the mass baptism because it seemed to validate and affirm that the Word was indeed spreading, and that converts were coming to help us build Christ's kingdom on earth.

The genesis of this mass baptism was in the research for *Reviving the Spirit*. And these candidates for baptism had come about as a result of evangelical efforts of Bethel AME and New Shiloh, another mega church, with more than eight thousand members. Bethel and New Shiloh had hosted an unusual Billy Graham–type crusade a month earlier at Oriole Park at Camden Yards in Baltimore—a three-day event that attracted 82,000 people. The jubilant services were described by the *Baltimore Sun* as a stadium of exasperated people engaged in a "giant primal scream." These fifty or sixty were among the hundreds who had responded to invitations by Reverend Reid and New Shiloh's Dr. Harold A. Carter to "join the church."

That night in Camden Yards, I saw just how much "the church" had changed. This day, at the baptism, I recognized how much things remained the same. I was encouraged by both the new and the old.

That religion is so attractive to so many younger people is reflective of our growing desire for a framework for living and worshipping. Most of us are simply trying to find balance between intellectual stimulation and emotional security.

With each baptism, we may be that much closer to reviving our churches.

Look to the rock from which you were cut and to the quarry from which you were hewn.

—Isaiah 51:1

The special strength of the black church has always been as a vehicle for social and political as well as spiritual transformation. At a time when America seeks ways to reinvent its national identity, to rehabilitate the spirits of alienated masses, to open the doors of opportunity for millions who feel locked out, black churches stand as institutions with a proven record in such transformation. Churches have demonstrated their capability for empowerment, emancipating black people from the ravages of generations of slavery and equipping them to recover a sense of identity, to forge ties of communal loyalty, to help themselves and others, and to create cultural expressions that embody their hopes and aspirations.

A Detroit News / Gannett News Service poll of 1,211 African Americans conducted a few years ago revealed that a majority believe that the black church is more effective at meeting their needs than the National Association for the Advancement of Colored People, the National Urban League, the Southern Christian Leadership Conference, or the Congress on Racial Equality. Add this to the multimillion-dollar investments in church buildings and other real estate holdings, and churches like Bethel become the most powerful economic force in black America.

> In the last days, God says, I will pour out my Spirit on all people. Your sons and daughters will prophesy, your young men will see visions, your old men will dream dreams.
>
> —Acts 2:17

My generation sees little separation between the traditional spiritual function of the church and the need for black political and economic parity. We are demanding that the black church—regardless of denomination—respond, or African Americans risk reenslavement on all fronts.

This decade will see greater efforts by churches like Bethel in organizing among the poor. The strategies for dealing with black children, teenagers, and young adults and their families will include a mix of traditional programs like youth choirs, evangelism, and revivals with progressive programs.

Today's ministry must preach that Money is God in action.

By "tithing" time and money, giving that biblically prescribed first 10 percent of their salary, "the first fruits of

Pooling resources may be the only means of building economic clout; it has proved to be the cornerstone of successful initiatives at some churches to empower their members economically. It is a strategy also advocated by Reverend W. Franklyn Richardson, general secretary of the National Baptist Convention, U.S.A., who is also pastor of Grace Baptist Church in Mt. Vernon, New York. "Our churches have millions of dollars invested in banks. We must ensure that banks reinvest in our communities," he told *Black Enterprise*.

Brooklyn's Concord Baptist Church, with pooled money, created Christfund, an endowment with $1 million raised by the congregation that is the source of grants to people or organizations that serve the immediate community. *Emerge* magazine reported that Christfund gave away $63,965 in 1989, its second year of service, to the Concord Nursing Home, the Billie Holiday Theater, the Brooklyn Academy of Music, and the public television series *Eyes on the Prize II*. "The idea of the Christfund is that we let money make money for Christ," says Concord minister Frederick C. Ennette.

Of black churches moving toward "hard" development, Wheat Street Baptist Church in Atlanta is considered one of the oldest models for economic activism. Since the 1960s, the church's nonprofit corporation, the Wheat Street Charitable Foundation, has developed two housing developments, several single-family dwellings, and two shopping centers built in 1969. With about fifteen hundred members, Wheat Street is considered by some as the wealthiest black church in America, with real estate holdings that exceed $33 million.

The church owns two strips in the heart of the Martin Luther King Jr. Center for Non-Violent Social Change that feature laundries, cleaners, restaurants, grocery stores, beauty shops, and an office building. Other properties include a fifteen-story, 496-unit senior citizen center and Wheat Street Gardens, a building with 496 low-income units. "The Lord's dominion is not limited to just what's inside the church," Reverend Michael Harris told *Black Enterprise*. "Before we can think in terms of heaven by and by, we've got to live here on earth. And Wheat Street, through its economic development projects, wants to make sure life on earth is as good as it can be."

In Philadelphia, the city's largest Pentecostal congregation, Deliverance Evangelistic Church, is building a shopping center to anchor the redevelopment of a distressed north Philadelphia neighborhood that was once home to the Connie Mack Stadium. The center is called Hope Plaza Shopping and is indicative of the new kind of community ministry being led by black clergy who find themselves developers of last resort in their home bases. Reverend Benjamin Smith, Deliverance's minister and chairman of Hope Plaza Inc., says, "You can't convince people their only need is spiritual when they are suffering financially. This is an effort to provide some jobs for our young people."

Bethany Baptist Church in Brooklyn, New York, used $1.5 million to open the 800-seat Harvest Manor Cafeteria and Banquet Center in a fire-gutted A&P grocery store. The center employs up to eighty people—primarily church members—and has served more than five thousand people in one week.

But not every economic venture being tried by churches is of the conventional sort. Mount Olivet Baptist Church in St. Paul, Minnesota, led by the Reverend James Battle, and a group of local businessmen bought 94.5 miles of railroad track between Norwood and Hanley Falls, Minnesota, for $1.8 million and formed what is believed to be the largest minority-controlled railroad company in the country. The group, called the Minnesota Valley Transportation Co., Inc., Southwest, bought the line from Chicago & Northwestern Transportation Co., which abandoned the track a few months earlier. "Just the rehabilitation program that we will soon have in place to work on the railroad tracks will provide fifty to sixty jobs. That's fifty to sixty families that will benefit. In all, the farms will be able to sell their grain to the local operators, and the operators will now have a railroad service to get their produce transported to other parts of the country," Reverend Battle said in *Ebony*.

The Christian Methodist Episcopal (CME) Church, a large, historically black denomination, raises money for its educational, social, and economic programs by sponsoring a national credit card. For every $3,000 spent by CME Affinity card holders, who number in the thousands, $20 goes to the denomination.

The spirit of God as money in action is not only an urban strategy; those in rural areas are embracing this self-help notion as well. At the Greater Christ Temple Church in Meridian, Mississippi, Bishop Luke Edwards, the church's pastor, believes in the power of pooled resources. When he founded the Pentecostal church in 1974, it had thirty-five members, 95 percent of whom were on welfare. Edwards got them to pool their food stamps and buy wholesale, and within four months the church was running a makeshift grocery store from the basement. In 1978 they parlayed that venture into an $18,000 purchase of a real grocery store, which they ran for a few years before selling it at a profit. Greater Christ Temple now operates three restaurants, a bakery, an auto repair shop, and a 4,000-acre farm with seven hundred head of cattle and two meat-processing plants. The members, now numbering two hundred, have been "delivered from welfare by pooling their resources," the pastor told *Ebony*. "Being black it's very difficult to get loans. We realized we had to turn to one another. We just had to work together."

Helping each other, pooling our pennies, and buying black are among the paths to progress cited in the results of the most recent National Survey of Black Americans, in which 89.8 percent felt we "should work together as a group," and 65 percent felt we should shop in black-owned stores.

Just as the civil rights movement was multi-pronged, so too is the current movement, in which the church is trying to become a leader, or at least a command center.

Driving this new movement is a population of pastors and parishioners who are better educated and more sophisticated and have far more political and economic clout than their predecessors. Our new church leaders fully recognize the power of ownership and entrepreneurship, and they realize that, given their collective money and expertise, they are in a unique position to jump-start their communities.

In Los Angeles, the 9,500-member First AME Church, considered an "economic lifeline" to its South Central neighborhoods, created the FAME Renaissance Program in the wake of the 1992 riots in the city. A $1 million grant from the Walt Disney Company led to the creation of the Micro Loan Program, which supplies low-interest loans of $2,000 to $20,0000 to minority entrepreneurs in the area. About thirty-four loans totaling $500,000 were approved within the first six months of the program. An additional grant to FAME from Atlantic Richfield Corp. of $500,000 is moving it toward the $10 million goal to fund at least one thousand new businesses. First AME hosts a ten-week entrepreneurial training program augmented by the congregation's talents. "Our membership has some three hundred attorneys, two hundred CPAs, and seven hundred business owners," Mark Whitlock, executive director of FAME, told *Black Enterprise.* "For every loan we make, the recipient also gets a mentor to help support that business. . . . Then we suggest to the congregation that they do business with the company owner we just made a loan to."

When churches wade into business waters, it is not always smooth sailing, however; there are ugly sides of business, too—late payments, defaulted loans, tensions over money.

"Being caught between two worlds," is how the Reverend Thomas Ritter described in the *New York Times* a decision in 1987 to evict a financially troubled, employee-owned supermarket from the Strawberry Square Mall in north Philadelphia that had opened in 1985 as a joint venture between a corporation affiliated with his Second Macedonia Baptist Church and a private developer.

The supermarket had defaulted on a $2.2 million bank loan. With a new supermarket in place, the mall developers found new financing. Generally, churches are protected from the financial problems of a project because deals are made through corporations that "borrow separately and distinctly from the church," said Robert L. Archie Jr., a lawyer for Deliverance Church in Philadelphia.

Aside from making risky loans, churches with tax-related businesses face questions about commingling of funds and unfair protection of tax revenue from the government. It is illegal for churches that operate as tax exempt to have an interest in a business that should rightly pay taxes on its revenues. Most churches, therefore, create foundations and community development corporations to run and administer their businesses.

These urgent needs in distressed black neighborhoods require coalitions of congregations so that their combined strengths and resources can more effectively serve their communities. Churches may find it strategically wise to join other religious or secular agencies—businesses, local and state governments, community-service agencies, foundations, and individuals—that share their mission and have the resources to make a significant impact.

Whether these thriving congregations offer encouraging models for the future will ultimately depend on those of us who have returned and make up the new congregations. Will African-American churches adjust to these revolutionary times, or will they become irrelevant?

If we chance it, we can provide employment opportunities, and our children can begin to acquire the skills that will take them up the economic ladder. Churches may not make a real dent in social problems, but the need to be a witness is vital.

> *The ransomed of the Lord will return. They will enter Zion with singing; everlasting joy will crown their heads.*
>
> —Isaiah 51:11

Black churches today are reviving the spirit of activism—the needed spark that has historically preceded significant leaps of progress for black people in American society.

We, the prodigal children, are forcing the black church to accept its role in a new black revolution. Our churches have started to reinterpret their mission—sermons and ministries—in terms of the needs of a black revolution for economic power.

My generation has always felt left out of the activism and synergy of the early sixties, but now in the 1990s, we are shaping our own movement for racial progress. The quest is the same: equality and self-determination. But the targets are not as easy to spy as segregated lunch counters, and the solutions are not as simple as sitting down. We are being beckoned to our meeting halls—the church—where we are regrouping and learning again how to speak a common tongue. At heart, we have learned that church remains the place to find the strength and courage to face down oppression all week, but increasingly we are no longer praying just for the strength to endure, we're praying for the strength to truly overcome.

ACKNOWLEDGMENTS

Many *angels* have helped to breathe life into this book, and I owe them many, many thanks.

In the beginning, there was Ilene Barth, who while at *Newsday* edited the original essay from which this book evolved under the patient guidance of Beth Vesel, my literary agent.

I am grateful to Bryan Oettel, who first acquired this book for Grove Press, and to my editor Jim Moser, who shaped its final form. To Rick Pracher I am grateful for this jacket's inspired cover image and to Linda Ainsworth for her fine transcription of taped interviews.

A special thanks to Arnetta Fowlkes, a member of Bethel AME Church in Baltimore, who first introduced me to Reverend Frank Madison Reid III. And to Rev. Reid and his family and congregation I am indebted, particularly to Pam Shaw, Patricia Wright, Larry Little, Leronia Josey, Sheila Dixon, Goldie Phillips, Vanda Guzman Perry, David

Perry and other members of Bethel's congregation who have shared the stories that make up this book.

My husband Calvin Perry Lawrence Jr.'s story is the real genesis of this work, and I can never repay him for his unconditional support. Special thanks to his wonderful parents, Ursula and Calvin Lawrence Jr., for providing me shelter and transportation during my visits in Baltimore.

I would like to thank my personal "ministers of mercy," chief among these my best friend, Bette Joan Wright. Others include Elaine Latzman Moon, Keith M. Holman, Diery Prudent, Sylvia Carter, Suzanne Curley, Beth Sherman, Cara DeSilva, Stanley Wolfson, Mike Dorman, Katti Gray, Nathan Jackson, Mira Thomas, Irene Sax, and Joan Kelly-Bernard.

A special thanks to my church families at Shiloh Baptist Church and the Highland Church in Jamaica, Queens. A special *gracias* to Pastor Frank Lorenzo, who revives my spirit each Sunday.